Whitewater Canoeing

Whitewater Canoeing

William O. Sandreuter

Winchester Press

Library of Congress Catalog Card Number: 75-34448
ISBN: 0-87691-223-4

Library of Congress Cataloging in Publication Data

Sandreuter, William O.
    Whitewater canoeing.
    Includes index.
    SUMMARY: Discusses the art of whitewater canoeing including trans-
porting and launching, maps and compass reading, canoe camping, and canoeing camps, schools, and competitions.
    1. White-water canoeing. [1. Canoes and canoeing] I. Title.
GV788.S26   797.1'22   75-34448
ISBN 0-87691-223-4

Published by Winchester Press
205 East 42nd Street
New York, N.Y. 10017

Printed in the United States of America

Acknowledgments

I EXTEND MY SINCEREST GRATITUDE to the many people who have contributed in numerous ways toward the completion of this book. Among those deserving special thanks are canoeing authorities Pierre Pulling and Payson Kennedy. Others most helpful were Ed Scofield, Angela Foote, Ned Lutz, Jan Kweit, and the book's editor, George Peper. I must also thank my wife Darleyne and children, Bill, Susan, Cindy, and Karl, who all helped with correspondence, photos, typing, and lots of other little important things.

I am particularly indebted to Joe Cole for his many action photos along the Nantahala River, to Clyde Smith for his action photos of the Upper Hudson and New Haven Rivers, and to Jim Foote who produced the equipment photos and provided me with technical advice for the pictures I took. Also of great assistance in this area were Larry McCarthy and Bill Donohue. My son Karl provided the photo of me on the jacket. Thanks also to Tim McGrath, Richard Tucker, Carl Chiapetta, David Henry, Alan Chidsey, and three nice guys from Brooklyn. Without the collective support of all these enthusiastic contributors, this book would not have been possible.

To my father, an avid outdoorsman who celebrated his 75th birthday on a 20-mile whitewater canoe trip. He showed me the way of the woods and the joy of canoeing.

Contents

Preface

MY FIRST IMPRESSION of the canoe's seaworthiness came when I was a young boy on Long Island Sound. I was with my father in his round-bottom sailer which is still in use. We were driving through six-foot seas off Greenwich Point, Connecticut, in a roaring gale with every fiber strained to its limit. We were sailing on a broad reach, and I was in the bottom of the canoe holding down the boom, bailing and trying to take strain off the lee rail leeboard as we drove forward determinedly through the angry seas. My father was perched on the stern seat, sheet in hand and holding a long paddle. He was a purist—no new-fangled canoe rudder for him. I remember glancing about as he sat steady and sure with his long-shafted paddle guiding us along. Occasionally a wave would crash over the side and sweep aft in a sheet of spray and foam. The salt always stung

my eyes, and after each wave I looked hard to see whether my
father was still at the helm.

I remember thinking he must be glued. I remember, also, his
smile which glowed warm through the water that dribbled
down his face and body. I wasn't scared and I worked furi-
ously to empty the sloshing water, hold the bottom down, and
take the strain off the leeboard.

Suddenly there was a crack like a firecracker. The leeboard
gave way to the ferocious sea. Our canoe halted, lurched sideways, swamped with water, and gently settled on its side. Dad
and I unstepped the mast, righted the craft, and treaded water
until we were picked up by a passing sailboat. Later we re-
covered the canoe from the shore where it had managed to
find shelter in a clump of tall grass.

I think of that exciting afternoon often when I am in those
same waters. I think of it especially when I am in the same
canoe, near the same clump of grass, plug-casting for bass on
a still moonlit night. I think of how gallantly it performed
and how unfortunate it was that the leeboard let go.

The canoe is by far the most magnificent water vehicle designed by man. Its long history goes back to primitive man who
constructed canoes from logs to give them safe passage through
dangerous swamps and forests. The Polynesians used canoes
for whaling and traveled great distances across the ocean, fishing and trading. American Indians made canoes from buffalo
hides and birch bark. Eskimos used single-man canoes fashioned
from sealskin for hunting, and the Norsemen traveled the
treacherous oceans in search of trade and natural resources
aboard huge canoes crafted from spruce and Nordic pine. Anywhere there is water, from the tropical lakes of Africa to the
ice-packed seas of the North, from the swift rivers of North
America to the islands of the Pacific, the canoe has served man
well. It is unbelievably seaworthy, swift, light, and for its size
it carries an impressive load.

I have known canoes all my life and I am fascinated by them.
But I am often annoyed by the way they are sometimes rep-

resented and the manner in which they are sometimes used. I have listened as spokesmen for responsible organizations have given bad impressions of the craft's seaworthiness. I know of groups that have insisted that the seats be removed from canoes because they believe sitting on them will turn the canoe over. I have even heard so-called experts say, "Never run white water; portage instead."

There are some people who just plain abuse canoes. They run them on the rocks, jump in and out of them, and eventually bang themselves up with them. I once found a little child floating in a canoe in the middle of a lake, with no paddle or life jacket, while the mother sunbathed on the beach. I have known of others who knew nothing about boating, let alone canoeing, who have gotten into canoes in their bare feet and run white water without life jackets. Two years ago, I saw a young couple, without life jackets, canoeing downriver from the Bushkill landing area on the Delaware River. They were headed for two groups of hazardous rapids, rated number 4 and number 5. In the center of the canoe was a baby about a year old lying on a blanket. We warned them about the dangers ahead, but they continued on. And although nothing happened in this case, it could have, and it often does happen to those who treat white water lightly.

The following pages reflect what I have learned in over 35 years of canoeing, from expert guides, instruction courses, and years of personal experience and teaching. I hope that I have presented the canoe as the stately lady she is. I hope, also, that I have provided answers to most of the questions people ask about whitewater canoeing. Finally, I hope the book is interesting, informative, and will lead the way toward many happy days with your canoe and the splendors of nature.

WILLIAM O. SANDREUTER
Old Greenwich, Connecticut
February 1, 1976

1

Kinds of Canoes

FOR CENTURIES CANOES HAVE BEEN made of such materials as hollowed-out logs, bark or skins over wood or bone frames, and even grass. Today most manufactured canoes are made of fiberglass, metal, or canvas over wood. We will discuss briefly these materials and such other factors as weight, shape, length, and depth. There are many types of canoes and they all seem to have characters and attributes of their very own. In order to choose the canoe that is best for you, you must first determine your needs. You must ask yourself where and why you will be using it.

If you expect to use your canoe only on a lake, you might enjoy the grace and charm of a wooden or canvas-over-wood canoe. If you plan to sail in it, you should probably go for a canoe with a round bottom. While it is not as stable as a flat-bottom canoe, it is a faster and superior sailer. If you have an eye for beauty, you will be hard pressed to resist one of the magnificent hand-crafted wooden canoes that are being built by several master craftsmen. They possess a great deal of sheer, and the lines are as beautiful as you will ever see. You might, however, become disenchanted with the high prow and aesthetic charm if you ever have a long way to paddle in a crosswind. Or perhaps you are looking for a canoe that you can use for racing. If this is the case, it's wise to seek out an expert racer, who will design and build a custom canoe to your requirements.

The three most popular materials used in canoe construction today are aluminum, fiberglass, and canvas over wood; the last, although it is a magnificent achievement of marine craftsmanship, should be ruled out for heavy whitewater running unless you are sure the river is deep and there is not much likelihood of damaging the skin or the bottom and ribs. Canvas over wood was used for years in white water before new and tougher materials came on the market, but today the time and cost of repairing and maintaining canvas-over-wood canoes make the aluminum and fiberglass models much more attractive. They can be stored most anywhere and need very little servicing. By comparison, a canvas canoe requires a new coat of canvas from time to time, and it takes patience and skill to do this job properly. Nevertheless, canvas canoes still have a large group of loyal supporters. There is a certain feel, a sort of live responsiveness, in a canvas canoe—a feeling I have never been able to experience in an aluminum or fiberglass model.

If your sole interest is white water, then by all means get a whitewater model designed for the rigors of the river. They are strong, and the aluminum models have additional thwarts and ribs. The fiberglass models can be purchased without a keel and the aluminum models can be purchased with a shoe keel designed expressly for white water. If you plan to use your canoe in a more general way, with only occasional white-water cruises, then a standard model manufactured by a re-

Two types of canoes popular among canoers today. The more traditional types are manufactured from fiberglass or aluminum. The sleek,
low-profile model, which is a delight on mild streams and quiet lakes,
is made of fiberglass.

liable company should fill your needs quite well. If your canoe
has a standard keel instead of the shoe keel you will not have
quite the same mobility or, more explicitly, the same capability
of slipping sideways that you would have without a keel or
with the shoe. This can be compensated for to some degree by
keeping the bow just a touch higher than the stern. It simply
puts less drag on the forward part of the keel and enables you
to move the bow over fairly fast to avoid an obstruction ahead.
   One important thing to check for when purchasing your

canoe is sufficient flotation. This is important in white water. A few manufacturers construct their canoes with only a minimum amount, barely enough to keep the canoe afloat. Grumman aluminum canoes have enough flotation in either end so that the canoe will right itself when upset. A heavy load of equipment, however, might prevent this, though the canoe will support the "in-water" weight of its maximum capacity. New on the market is the Browning AeroCraft Fox. Pliable nonabsorbent flotation foam is specially bonded to the hull of this aluminum canoe under the gunwale both inside and out. The beam on the Fox is wider than most 17-foot canoes, and web seats, designed so that your feet will not get caught while kneeling, also establish a lower center of gravity because they are positioned lower than those of some other manufacturers.

Consideration certainly has to be given to the weight and length of a canoe. Weight, of course, is pretty much determined by the material from which the canoe is manufactured. Generally, aluminum is the lightest, but, surprisingly, the new fiberglass models are not all that much heavier. They also have several excellent features that make choosing between them and aluminum very difficult. The Old Town Canoe Company of Old Town, Maine, is using a new material known as vinyl-ABS-foam. It is exceptionally strong and almost indestructible; besides that, the consistency of the foam sandwich is such that it provides flotation throughout. Also, dents can be removed by heating. Aluminum, of course, is durable and safe and is quite resistant to puncture and dents, due to a marine aluminum alloy and heat-treated parts. Like the vinyl-ABS, it requires very little maintenance.

Grumman manufactures both standard and lightweight canoes. They range in size from 15 to 18 feet in length and have an average beam of just over 36 inches. The average depth is just over 13 inches. The standard model uses .050-inch gauge aluminum while the lightweight model uses .032-inch gauge aluminum reinforced with extra ribs. The regular keel model (best for lakes) is $\frac{5}{8}$-inch deep, and the shallow-draft shoe-

The Old Town vinyl-ABS foam canoe making a run as the bow man cross draws to assist in redirecting the craft.

keel craft is ⅜-inch deep (best for rivers). The average weight of the standard 17-foot Grumman aluminum canoe runs 75 pounds while the 17-foot lightweight weighs 60 pounds.

It is interesting to note that the new Old Town vinyl-ABS-foam sandwich canoe is quite competitive weightwise. The standard 16-foot model weighs 65 pounds and the standard 18-footer weighs 75 pounds. However, both these models do have about an inch less depth than the Grumman.

Old Town also manufactures a fiberglass canoe with a balsa-sandwich construction in the bottom which permits flexing and gives it the feel of a wooden canoe (well, almost). It

The versatile aluminum Grumman being piloted by a single paddler through a tricky race course.

is very stable and comes with a molded-in keel unless you specify that you would prefer it without. It comes in several lengths, from 11 feet, 11 inches to 18 feet. One model, the 17-foot, 2-inch Voyageur, has a width of 37 inches and a depth of 15 inches. It is excellent for crusing the river with heavy loads. It weighs only 74 pounds but the present cost is $425 F.O.B.

To compete pricewise and weightwise with the 17-foot Grumman aluminum, standard shallow-draft model which weighs 81 pounds, Old Town makes a less expensive standard 16-foot Carleton fiberglass canoe that weighs 79 pounds but has a 12-inch depth as against a 13½-inch depth for the aluminum. Its price is $375. The cost of the Grumman is $359.

Although most aluminum canoes are cheaper than the fiberglass, the costs are fairly competitive among manufacturers. It should also be noted that, regardless of materials, there is very little difference in cost between a 15- and 17-foot canoe. As an example, a large nationally known outfitter is currently advertising the 17-foot standard Grumman aluminum for $328 F.O.B. The 15-foot standard model sells for $310 F.O.B. Two extra feet of canoe cost a mere $18—a real bargain in today's market.

In the same catalog, the 16-foot Old Town Chipewyan with the vinyl-ABS-foam is selling for $395 F.O.B. The 14-foot model is selling for $375 F.O.B. The Old Town 16-foot fiberglass Carleton model, as mentioned already, is selling for $375 and the 14-footer for $355. In today's market these prices could change drastically, but the main point here is to show the cost relationship between materials as well as between sizes of canoes.

There are many canoe manufacturers, both in this country and Canada and Europe, who manufacture fine products. Black River Canoes of Lagrange, Ohio, manufactures nine models from 10 feet, 3 inches to 18 feet, 6 inches. They claim they make the best canoes in the country. I mentioned Old Town and Grumman here strictly to make comparisons between costs, sizes, and materials. They are well known and manufacture excellent products. For this reason, I selected them for this study.

The canvas-over-wood canoe is still obtainable from a few manufacturers, and costs generally run more than the fiberglass. When new they weigh about the same as the aluminum, but you must remember, if you plan to buy one, to allow for moisture and the accumulation of paint and varnish if weight is a factor. Over the years your canoe could gain 20 pounds from paint and over the summer, under certain conditions, 20 pounds from moisture. Naturally the latter would not be as severe if care were taken to properly protect the canvas and interior of the canoe, and if it were not left in the rain or subjected to frequent duckings. Even though these factors might be considered drawbacks there are, in the town of Charlotte, Vermont, just below Burlington on Lake Champlain, several master craftsmen who have been busy over recent years reviving the art of building wooden and canvas canoes.

There are smaller 14- and 15-foot canoes made of the same basic materials mentioned, and they are, of course, proportionately light but not by much. Figure a difference of about 5 to 10 pounds for each additional foot of canoe. Be cautious when buying a short canoe, and don't do it just for reasons of weight. I believe that in white water the 16- and 18-foot canoes respond better to the challenge. They seem to hold their course better, are more resistant to crosscurrents, and generally give a smoother ride. For lake travel, I also prefer the longer canoes because they seem to move along with greater strength and balance. It is true that the extra weight and length can be difficult for young people to handle, especially when launching and on a portage. Some argue that the shorter length allows young people to get the canoe to respond more quickly for the limited amount of energy they are able to expend on a maneuver, but I feel that because the ride is bumpier in a 14- or 15-footer on white water, the canoe is more difficult to control.

Fourteen-footers and even 12s are ideal for fishing on a small pond or exploring narrow, winding streams. For a single person they also have advantages. If you plan to tote your canoe on top of a Volkswagen or Honda Civic, it might also be to your advantage to look at the shorter models. Some children's camps also like the small canoes for teaching, and, of course, they present less of a problem when it comes to storage. On the river or the lake, however, particularly if you're on a camping trip, the 16- to 18-footers are preferable in my opinion.

Width and freeboard are also factors to be considered when choosing a canoe. Freeboard is the least amount of hull out of water from the water line to the gunwale. I prefer a 36-inch width or beam and 14-inch depth, which should provide a minimum 12-inch freeboard. Some canoe manufacturers try to cut down on weight by making their canoes narrower at the ends, giving them less beam, reducing the freeboard, or effecting a combination of the three. This is true primarily among some fiberglass manufacturers, who want to be competitive weightwise with the aluminum canoe makers. Unless they are designing a canoe for specific needs, it really doesn't seem practical to me to sacrifice the finer attributes of this craft for the sake of weight. Scaling down such as this could lower the load capacity by well over 100 pounds.

This is not to say that for certain needs, a narrow-beam, low-profile canoe would not be desirable. On a windy lake it would be delightful. It would also be an advantage for fishing where you would not want to have a lot of the hull exposed to the breeze while at your favorite pool or log. Naturally a beamy canoe with good freeboard can carry a respectable load, some-

Fiberglass canoe with straight-cut bow, minimum sheer, and a fair amount of freeboard. This style bow may not be as forgiving as the more conventional kind.

where in the neighborhood of 700 or 800 pounds. That is certainly a much larger capacity than you need even with two 200-pound paddlers. Remember, however, that you may be carrying a passenger and this, combined with additional gear, would bring you close to maximum capacity, which would not be desirable, especially on white water.

There are a few manufacturers who turn out a canoe that is fairly wide amidships (the middle), then tapers rather sharply fore and aft. If you plan only lake paddling, this style might be worth considering since it does move through the water swiftly and with ease. It knifes through the waves similarly to the way a destroyer parts the seas, and this is fine as long as the waves are not too high. Don't confuse this, however, with some models which have a slightly outward flare to the hull. This small bulge is designed to deflect the water and keep the canoe drier.

For sailing, if that is your pleasure, the narrower round-bottom canoe seems to be best, provided, of course, it is equipped with leeboards (boards which attach to the canoe to prevent sideslip).

For general all-round use, especially on the river, the broad-beamed, fuller, flat-bottom model is the best, depending upon the size, material, and manufacturer's personal touches. It may be a little slower and it may not look as graceful as some of the sleeker whitewater models, with a rocker profile (bow and stern curve upward), but it can carry a huge load, paddles easily, and is a tough, unyielding, seaworthy craft in even the roughest conditions. There are very few 16- or 18-foot runabouts, skiffs, or ski boats that will stand up to the standard, full-beamed, flat-bottom 16- or 18-foot canoe in the hands of skilled paddlers against turbulent seas.

Finally, if only to emphasize the versatility of the magnificent canoe, I should mention the modern version of the Indian pack canoe. It is manufactured by Old Town, is made of fiberglass, and weighs only 19½ pounds. It is ideal for one man, not only for exploring streams and fishing but also as a dinghy.

Eric Amundsen, proprietor of southwestern Connecticut's headquarters for Grumman, Old Town, and Mallard canoes, in Old Greenwich, holds a 19-pound single-man pack canoe. It is ideal for small streams and ponds and can also serve well getting to and from the moorings. It has a styrofoam seat, and the thwart is constructed in the shape of a carrying yoke for portage.

It can be poked in the rear of a station wagon, tossed on top of the car, or carried a goodly distance on its built-in carrying yoke by a very young youngster. It's a remarkably stable and swift little craft and is simply ideal for that spur of the moment desire to go afloat.

Two popular canoes, a Grumman and an Old Town ABS, side by side. Under severe conditions and in the hands of equally competent paddlers, the deeper Grumman would probably ship less water and rise to the occasion swifter than the Old Town. On the other hand, the Old Town ABS, with its flat, keelless bottom, would respond more quickly in a lateral move and would be more forgiving sliding off a rock.

Again let me say that it is not easy to select the proper canoe, and since the cost is substantial I would suggest that you rent several different models, if possible, before making a choice. I recommend this because I myself find it difficult to select the best canoe for all conditions. For example, I personally feel that the Old Town vinyl-ABS-foam canoe does not rise

For both kayakers and canoers the Romer helmet shown here is excellent. It is durable and light, and on the chin strap is a chin cup for support. Shown here also are knee pads for the canoer, gloves, and life jacket.

to the occasion as quickly as a Grumman aluminum of approximately the same length. As a result we take in more water in heavy conditions unless my son moves aft from the bow seat to just in front of the center thwart. For slithering over the tops of rocks, however, the Old Town ABS is much more forgiving than the aluminum which, at times, tends to stick.

Whatever canoe you choose, you should consider adding a couple of accessories for white water. The Nantahala Outdoor Center in Wesser, North Carolina, has come up with an excellent idea for providing added buoyancy and rigidity, in case your canoe meets broadside with a rock. A block of Styrofoam is placed in the hull. The thwarts which have been removed are placed in the grooves of the Styrofoam and refastened to their normal position. The block is about four feet in length and extends from gunwale to gunwale. It rises two inches above the gunwales so that the canoe can be transported on the top of a car without a rack. The tie lines can run through the open windows. This added precaution of the Styrofoam reduces damage considerably and can keep you going with a considerable amount of water in the canoe.

Among the other accessories you may wish to consider if you are planning whitewater trips is the spray cover which fits over the bow. You may wish to purchase helmets as well, but you should have no need for such items until after you have mastered all of the basics.

2

From Home to Water: Transporting and Launching

ONE OF THE REASONS that the canoe has always been a popular water vehicle is, of course, the ease with which it can be carried about. Because it is light, it can be carried easily by a reasonably strong adult and it will even ride on the top of a Volkswagen bug. Two can be carried on the top of your car as easily as two pair of skis.

There are also trailers that can transport up to 20 canoes behind your car. Many canoe clubs like the convenience of being able to haul their canoes in this manner. For short trips and for outfitters, this is a good means of transport, but if you have to travel more than 30 or 40 miles, it can be a nuisance. On the open highway you must be careful of crosswinds and must travel at a very moderate rate. On country roads you must watch the bumps and be careful of the sway caused by high crowns in the road. Also, there are those unfortunate times when the car or trailer that is carrying the canoes breaks down 20 miles from your destination.

The method I prefer most is to carry two canoes atop each car. This saves a lot of disappointment and shares the responsibility more equitably. I have never felt comfortable hauling a load of canoes by trailer and when you finally arrive at the river, you invariably are greeted with scowls and remarks that insinuate that you must have stopped at least 20 times along the way for coffee or stopped at all the hardware stores. With the roof racks it's easier to keep together and everyone arrives at about the same time. To avoid criticism, I have often left an hour earlier with a trailer, but you find this doesn't help because you spend it trying to grope your way through the fog. When you get out of it, your friends sail past and figure you only left five minutes ahead of them, not the hour ahead you promised.

If your wagon is equipped with a full roof rack, two spruce two by threes, each five feet long, may be secured to the rack, and the canoes may be positioned on top. Securely tie each canoe separately to the crossbars.

Bow and stern lines should be placed as shown to prevent shifting. Caution should be taken to pad the line against sharp surfaces.

There are many new racks on the market but I still like a good substantial one that clamps securely to the car's gutter with turnbuckles and strong hooks that really grip. Single racks can be expanded to hold two canoes by lashing, or preferably, bolting, two spruce two-by-threes to the single rack. I like to lash them down. If I'm carrying two, I lash them down independently and I use good quarter-inch line of manila, dacron, or nylon. Never use clothesline, and make sure that whatever you use is not rotten. Remember that the line might tie all right, but one bad spot in a high wind can send the canoe soaring into the air. There are on the market today racks that have clamps that attach to the gunwale. They are

If you carry along an extra pair of crossbars and some extra line you might be able to assist a friend, but be sure the crossbars are secure as well as the canoe.

At a reasonable rate of speed, this rig works well.

fine provided you tie the canoe on as well. I shudder at the thought of a canoe flying off through someone's windshield.

When you position your rack on the top of the car, keep the crossbars as far apart as possible without affecting their

The VW bug can carry a canoe anywhere, provided the craft is properly secured fore and aft and is in the middle of a sturdy roof rack. The line for tieing down should be strong, quarter-inch manila, nylon, or dacron—not clothesline. The line should be protected from chafing, and the knots must be secure.

angle. Make sure they are secured properly to the gutter. After you get the canoes on top, check again and you will probably find you can take up a little slack. If your rack has suction cups, make sure the surface is clean before you try to get them to stick. Use plenty of water and make sure they are not all dried out or bent. Do not depend upon them for any more than just a bearing surface, as the rack is held by the tie-downs. I like to tie the thwarts to the rack. This prevents shifting. Next, cross-tie the bow to the frame underneath the bumper. If you plan a lot of canoe hauling, bore holes in the bumper and insert eyebolts. Never tie onto the bumper where the oscillations on the line will cause it to be cut through by the sharp edge of the bumper. Check that the rack is on properly and the canoe is properly balanced; most of it should be up front hanging over the front hood. There should not be very

If you travel at a reasonable speed it is even possible to carry two canoes atop a VW bug. Be sure both canoes are secure, and always run separate lines to the various tie-down points. If you do not wish to cut the line, tie and loop it in such a way that one break will not send the canoe flying.

much hanging over the road behind unless the car is small or you have a large canoe. Here, again, use a crisscross tie-down to prevent shifting. Eyebolts should be used here also on some part of the frame where you will get the least amount of chafing. It's a good idea, if you are not using eyebolts, to use some sort of chafing pad. I once saw a fellow tie his canoe onto his license plate fore and aft. It is always a good idea to hang a red flag in the rear just in case the fellow behind you is distracted by something along the edge of the highway. After you are secure, check the lines again to make sure there is no movement sideways or up and down. When you stop for a rest be sure to check your load and lines again.

Once you've reached your river, be sure to pick a good

A good way to store canoes.

launching site. Stay clear of steep banks, fast-moving water, mud, and brambles. Allow for plenty of room on the river to get organized before you plunge off into white water.

I always try to find access near a large pool where I can shake out the wrinkles and gain back my sea legs. A few minutes of this practice paddling can pay off in many ways. It gets you and your partner familiar with each other's movements, and, like warming up before a tennis match, it puts you in stride.

A large pool is also a good place to check out any new members of your group. Be sure they have full command of their canoe before shoving off downstream. Don't canoe with anyone you feel is not qualified for the section of the river you plan to travel. If you have beginners in your group, let them go as passengers but not in command of their own canoe. If you have a couple of exceptionally good canoers, try to split them up by having each one take a beginner with him and letting the beginner paddle from the bow seat.

When you place the canoe in the water, be sure that it is floating properly and not teetering on the shore before you enter. I like sliding the canoe into the water bow first so that there is no jockeying around. If you are launching eight or ten canoes, launching stern first could cause a lot of congestion. There is another very good reason for launching bow first: The bow man's paddling position is closer to the center of the canoe than that of the stern man. This, of course, means better balance when the stern man enters. A good practice is to have the stern man hold the canoe steady between his knees as the bow man moves forward to his position. The paddles, which we will discuss in the next chapter, should already be in the canoe. Once in place, the bow man, kneeling, can take his paddle and place it straight down over the side, close to the thwart, and steady the canoe so that the stern man can enter. As with any small boat, always remember when you step in to place your foot in the center of the canoe over the keel.

If the area where you are launching is stony and rough, you

Canoe is placed in the water bow first.

By passing the canoe forward as illustrated you avoid scraping the bottom.

The stern man steadies the canoe as the bow man makes his way forward in the center of the canoe, holding onto the gunwales.

can save scratching up the bottom of the canoe by having the canoers pick up the canoe on either side by the gunwales at the balance point and then passing it hand over hand into

The bow man, in position, steadies the canoe with his paddle so that the stern man can enter.

The stern man shifts his weight so that the canoe floats free, and the canoers begin to paddle.

the water above the ground. You may be able to find a launch area only where there is a current running. If this is the case, drop the canoe into the water with the bow facing upstream or as far up as you can get it for a clear departure. If you are launching your canoe from a dock, again, lift it at the balance point and work it hand over hand into the water with your partner. Be sure, though, that someone remembers the painter so that the canoe doesn't float off.

When you get in, be sure the canoe is parallel to the dock. With one person holding the canoe in the middle, the other should step into the center of the canoe and assume his position. He in turn steadies the canoe against the dock while his partner enters. Be sure the painters are coiled and secured with a large elastic band or such before departure.

I recall a time I was with a group of Boy Scouts at a launch area on the Delaware. There were some young boys along, full of excitement and hopeful that they could meet the challenge. Into our midst at a slow trot came a stocky, bewhiskered giant with his canoe. He flipped that canoe down from his shoulders and into the river as if he were lowering a bag of feathers. The boys were very impressed and a few, I am sure, felt slightly intimidated. In a flash, and without so much as a glance at his craft or the boys, he made his way back to the car, this champion of the river, to gather the rest of his gear— while his canoe slid silently downstream without him.

When you are coming in from the river for a landing, try to pick a place where you are sheltered from the current and there is sand as opposed to rock and mud. Pick a place where the bank is not too steep or littered with overhanging branches and fallen dead trees. If the water is moving swiftly, try to back into an eddy (water moving back upstream), so that you do not get your canoe sideway across the current, which could swamp you if you get hung up on the rocks. Surprising as it may seem, this is usually the time when people get into the most trouble. Sometimes when tired, the idea of stopping is foremost in your mind and causes you to forget that the river runs on and is still anxious to provide challenges. If you must stop along the bank in a swift current, stay in line with it and pull into the bank either backward or forward but remaining pointing downriver. The stern man can secure the stern painter to a branch on the bank and the bow man can then do the same. Your canoe should not offer much resistance to the river due to the shape of the stern which will allow the water to flow past easily unless the flow is excessive. If you have no choice and there are lots of stones, it is best to get out of the canoe with your shoes on and walk the craft to shore. Aside from the fact that deck shoes or felt soles will keep you from slipping on the rocks, they may also keep you from cutting your feet on a broken bottle or can, left by some thoughtless person.

3

Paddles and Paddling

Paddles

THERE ARE PROBABLY AS MANY opinions about paddles as there
are about skis or hiking shoes. Without getting too complex,
I will point out what I consider to be the main features to keep
in mind when selecting paddles. Style, material, size, and
width all are important in selecting the right paddle, but what
counts most is being able to handle that paddle under difficult
conditions.

Some paddles are made of plastic, others of different kinds
of wood. Some are laminated, some aren't. Let us discuss

wooden paddles first. For general rough paddling on the river, it is difficult to beat the sturdiness of maple. Although it is heavier than ash or spruce, maple has a ruggedness that is well worth the price you pay in extra weight. Ash is lighter, more flexible, and nearly as rugged, but I always feel better with maple in white water. Spruce is by far the lightest but, of course, it lacks the durability of either maple or ash. In calm water or on a still, misty morning, it is a delight to use a spruce paddle as you coast along plug-casting for bass.

Be careful when you are buying a paddle that you are really buying a device that will propel your canoe through the water without breaking your back. There is a lot of timber sold to-day in the shape of paddles. Examine the paddle carefully. Be sure the shaft or loom, as it is sometimes called, is straight, not bowed or hooked. Check the grain of the shaft and be sure it is fairly straight and free of knots. Next check the blade. First, see that it isn't lopsided, warped, or hooked. Then check its edge and weight to be sure it is not too fat or heavy. The quality of some of the paddles placed on the shelves today is shock-ingly poor, and it can be a very disappointing experience to end up on the river with a huge wooden spoon. Even if you are renting a canoe, be sure that they give you a spare and that the blade is not split. Paddles are like shoes, they must fit; if they don't, they can cause a lot of pain. Earlier I mentioned laminated paddles. Most of the good ones are quite strong, but they do not seem to have the same spring and resilience that the maple or ash paddle has.

Another factor to keep in mind is the width of the blade. Paddles come in widths of anywhere from five to nine inches. Naturally, the narrow blade pulls through the water with greater ease, and is of great advantage to a younger person or someone with short arms. For either the youngster or the short-armed adult, the narrow blade is better because, to keep on a straight course, the paddler must pull straight back with his paddle parallel with the keel. If the blade is too wide, this particular paddler will pull off the line and follow the gun-

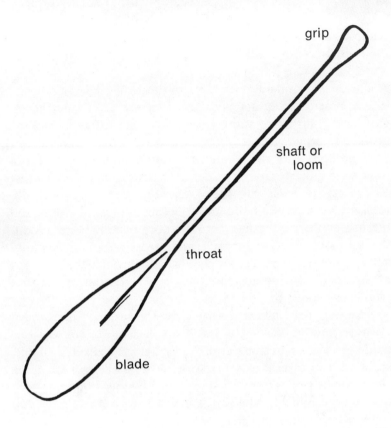

grip

shaft or
loom

throat

blade

wale angle. Such a stroke will, of course, cause the canoe to respond by going off at an angle to the opposite side of the paddler. This, of course, could be corrected by the stern man, but the effort of canoeing is far easier if both paddlers are pulling together in a straight line that parallels the keel. The ride is much easier and smoother.

In a tight spot, however, if you put your muscle into a wide blade, you will get more immediate thrust and your canoe will respond more quickly. I prefer a 7- or 8-inch blade, especially on the river. One good sweep with a blade of this width is usually enough to keep me riding on a course through the vees. It is more efficient, I believe, provided you have the muscle to handle it.

The next consideration is the length of the shaft, but, again, this is a personal preference. You can use your own height arm length as guides, and buy a paddle that extends from the ground to somewhere between the shoulder and the top of your head. Within these limits, the bow man usually prefers a somewhat shorter paddle, provided it has enough shaft so that he can really dig it into the water. The stern man normally finds a longer paddle more useful because he can dig deep and the longer shaft gives him better rudder power. With a long-shafted paddle, he can gently paddle from a standing position and get himself lined up for the descent through the next run of rapids. (I can just imagine what some canoe-safety experts would say about this one.)

I remember the first time that I saw this little act performed. I was somewhat startled as I saw our heretofore conservative guide, who was threading us down the Alagash River in Maine, stand up and as neat as you please, lead us all right onto the conveyor belt of water that leaped and bounced down a difficult watery hill. He took his seat just before we felt the full force of the river, and away we all went.

Later when I asked him if he always did that and did he consider it safe, he looked at me, contemplated his answer and eventually spoke. "Son," he said, taking a draw on his pipe, "I ask ya, how ya gonna see down those stairs theya less ya stand up theya and take a look round? This river heaz betta some days on the left, others on the right. I want ta know where I am going fore I gets committed." I replied that I could understand that all right but still questioned the wisdom of standing in a canoe and possibly ending in the drink. I told him what my camp counselor had told me about such actions. The old man, or at least I thought he was old because I was just seventeen, took a long slow drag on his pipe again, looked up, and let the smoke out real slow. This he spoke. "Why, course it's all right ta stand up. It's the natural thing ta do. Just cuz them fellas down Philadelphia say t'aint don't mean t'aint." I didn't know what he meant about them Philadelphia fellas because I didn't know anyone from Philadelphia and had never been there. I didn't pursue it anymore.

Next time I had the opportunity, though, I gave standing up a try. It was easy, the natural thing to do. It is safe and it does put you in a good position to read the river and line yourself up for what's ahead. As long as you are in a flat-bottomed canoe and your bow man remains seated or on his knees, there is no danger. It is a decided advantage. Just don't do it in swift running water or where there are lots of boulders just under the surface. Exercise a little caution and you will have no trouble. If you know the river well enough so that you don't have to get out and examine every rapids, it's a great way to make a check of the known trouble spots and avoid possible mishaps.

In recent years they've come up with an aluminum-shafted paddle with a fiberglass blade. I have used it and it is not bad. It is quite light and for this reason seems to attract young people who prefer them to the wood. My only real complaints with it are that the handle sometimes begins to wiggle with age, the aluminum stains the hands, and I have had difficulty finding one with a long enough shaft to meet my requirements for a stern paddle. I am inclined to believe that you are slightly more blister-prone when using the aluminum paddle but this is more opinion than actual fact. On the subject of blisters, it should be mentioned that you can get badly blistered up on a wooden handle if it doesn't fit your hand right, and especially if the shaft and handle grips are varnished. If possible, always remove the varnish from the grips, rub the wood down, and then rub it with a little boiled linseed oil. Strange as it may

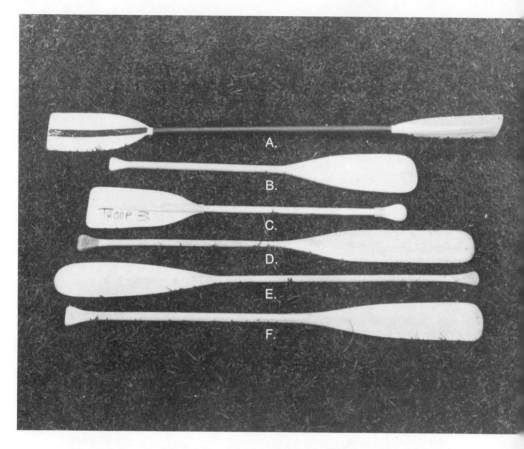

A: Fiberglass double blade, scooped, on light metal shaft. B: Laminated maple with broad blade, round shaft, and flared grip. C: Blade of plastic material on round aluminum shaft. D: Oil-rubbed ash with beaver-tail blade, round shaft, and flared-T grip. E: Maple with round Maine-guide blade, round, slender shaft, and small, more rounded grip. F: Ash with squared-off blade, flat, oval shaft, and flat, flared-T grip. There are many variations of the above, made of different materials and with modified grips. A paddle is a very personal thing.

seem, a nice, smooth, varnished handle can provide you with a very ugly hand at the end of the day.

Always be sure that the handle grip fits your hand, that it is not too fat or slim. There are various types of handles, and I suppose they all work well under certain conditions, but I consider the flat flared-T grip to be the best. It feels firm in the hand. You know from the grip exactly how the blade of your paddle is angled and because it is not fastened onto the shaft but rather a part of it, it cannot work loose. Some grips have rounded tops, others have regular handles that resemble shovels, but the best one I know for serious canoeing is the flat flared-T grip.

Blades vary in shape also, from the beaver-tail and Maine-guide-types to the square blade. I would make a choice between the square blade and the Maine guide. If you have the power, the square blade is certainly efficient in most water. In really swift rapids, however, it can be difficult to move about quickly. In heavy water, I would lean toward the Maine-guide cut. Regardless of which blade design you select, be sure that the shape is even, not too fat, and uniformly tapered to a clean, thin edge.

I know of several people who enjoy taking along with them on milder rivers, rated 2 or 3, double-blade paddles about ten feet in length. They are available in either flat blade or spoon and can be gotten in two sections. I am not particularly a booster of the double paddle for river cruising in white water because I feel, for one thing, that conventional paddles present far fewer problems when maneuvering through tight quarters. They are efficient and essential for some types of racing and do, without question, add a slightly different dimension to canoeing. If you feel you really must have one, then get the flat blade which responds better in white water.

Remember always that your paddle is your propeller and it must not be used as a lever to get off the rocks unless the situation is critical. It should not normally be used as a pole either, to push you over a shoal into deeper water. If you should find yourself in this situation, get out and walk your craft until it will carry you again. Abuse like this could break the handle or split the blade. In most cases, you can make emergency repairs, but it is best to carry a spare paddle or two.

Sitting and Kneeling

Before you can paddle, you must be able to assume a comfortable and effective position in the canoe. Basically, you can either sit or kneel, and often your position will depend on the design of the canoe.

Some canoes have raised seats flush with the gunwale; others have seats that are lowered. There are many canoes with no seats at all, and some camp directors remove seats from standard models for, as they put it, "maximum safety." In their place, they add additional thwarts. To sit on these is unwise. You can lose your balance quickly, get hurt, and even capsize the canoe. Moreover, perching on a thwart doesn't enable you to put as much power into your stroke.

I prefer a canoe with seats, simply because they are more comfortable. I do not subscribe at all to the possible safety hazards seats can cause. There is, however, one manufacturer who places extra braces under the seats which, if you are in a kneeling position, could cause you difficulty getting your feet out should the canoe go over.

There are many variations on kneeling which call for one leg up, knees apart, etc. There are many variations for racing with one leg extended forward. The Indians developed a squat where you can sit on the inside of your ankles, but I wouldn't try this one for any extended period unless I had first acquired a lot of practice. The important considerations are safety, comfort, and control. If you plan to spend much time in your canoe, you should mix it up and not stay in any one position

When paddling a canoe by yourself, sit in the bow seat facing aft, and paddle stern-first. The canoe doesn't mind, and as you can see it rides very well in the water.

too long. It is less fatiguing if you change around. When sitting, find a comfortable position with your knees apart. The same is true when kneeling; keep your knees apart—it will give you better balance and enable you to get a better bite on the water with your paddle. Bracing with the knees is necessary when sitting as well as kneeling, and care should be taken, when cementing in knee pads, that they are properly positioned.

The only advice about sitting versus kneeling is to sit only when you are coasting along or cruising in calm water. Your center of gravity is higher in this position and you create greater wind resistance. Kneeling on both knees is perfect for

Properly sitting in the canoe, the paddlers are able to maintain good balance even while they scull their craft sideways.

white water or pushing along swiftly in calmer waters. When you are in the kneeling position your body is able to put more into the stroke. In this position you are using your thigh muscles and trunk muscles along with your arms and shoulders. In effect, you have more parts working toward moving you through the water and therefore you should find it less tiring. Whether sitting or kneeling, you must always be careful to stay clear of any loose lines, and don't get in a position where you can become wedged between the thwarts or seats if the canoe capsizes.

There are many different techniques for paddling a canoe.

In the kneeling position and braced against the seats, the paddlers are able to apply a great deal more force and leverage in moving their canoe.

Kneeling provides much greater leverage when applying the brakes or moving the canoe sideways.

Some of them are excellent, others are tiring and not very efficient. Paddling a canoe all day long through an unrelenting headwind can be a chore, but if you follow a few basic rules such as paddling in the lee of the land (sheltered from the wind), keeping off the seats so that you cut down the wind resistance, and making an effort to pull steadily, cleanly, and in unison, your day's journey will not be hard.

As you place yourself in the canoe, take the hand on the side you want to paddle and grip the paddle by the throat. Your other hand reaches across the front of your body and forward, and grasps the grip of the paddle on top. When you reach forward to set your paddle in the water and pull, the blade should be immersed deep enough to get a good bite on the water. At least three-quarters of the blade should be pulling.

The cruising stroke is, as the words imply, the stroke used

The paddle is shown here in action. The bow man reaches forward to set his blade. The center paddler has just completed a stroke, and the stern man has his paddle set deep as he completes a forward draw.

for cruising or pulling the canoe through the water. The bow man reaches forward with his paddle and pulls back through the water parallel with the keel until the paddle is even with the side of his body. Eventually, as you gain confidence, you will want to give a final thrust with the paddle before lifting it out of the water and moving it forward again. Those of you who have rowed a boat should be aware of the advantages of being able to feather the oars on the backswing, especially in a headwind. The canoe paddle can be feathered in much the same manner. As you pull the paddle from the water, twist your wrists forward and swing the blade of the paddle forward just above the water until you are ready to dig in for the next stroke. This saves a lot of unnecessary bending and lifting, which looks rather sloppy from the shore. A pair of good paddlers make it all look quite effortless. The thing that both paddlers must learn in the beginning is to pull in a straight line. Usually when the bow jerks from one side to the other, it is because someone is not pulling correctly.

For this maneuver as well as most maneuvers, the stern man should paddle on the opposite side, reaching forward simultaneously with the bow man and pulling back with him. Paddling should, for the most part, be a harmonious movement.

It may be discovered between the two paddlers that one or the other may have to pull with a little less force to keep the canoe on a straight course. Working together is the key to good paddling, with both paddlers mindful of each other's actions. A word of caution might be interjected here, and that is the same that applies to any inexperienced hiker or climber. Pace yourself. Start off slowly and don't try to see how fast you can go. A gentle, steady stroke will move you through the water with surprising swiftness and it will leave you pleasantly tired at the end of the day rather than totally exhausted. Switch from side to side occasionally and from time to time pull into the shore and switch from bow to stern. Don't stay riveted to your seat either. Mix it up. Sit when you can, and when you are working the rapids, kneel with your knees apart on a kneeling pad. I prefer a wide, thick foam pad similar to the ones used for gardening. It should be cemented to the floor and sides of the canoe. The kind that attach to the knee like basketball players wear can, after a few hours, cause irritation behind the knees and they get lost quite easily, but they are good if you must shift position frequently.

Paddling a canoe should be a relaxing, enjoyable experience. If it becomes work, you are paddling too hard. As you begin to get the knack of this basic forward stroke, you will find that by using the hand that grips the throat of the paddle as a fulcrum or pivot and by pushing with your upper hand, the effort of paddling becomes even less.

The stern man is principally responsible for steering the canoe, and there are several methods of combining the paddle stroke with steering. Some work well and others, like the common J stroke, have, in my estimation, certain faults. The J stroke tends to slow the canoe and, I feel, over a long period of time it becomes tiring and awkward. There are modifications of this stroke, but I feel the most practical method of guiding the canoe from the stern is what I like to call the draw feather stroke. If this stroke is done correctly, it takes little more effort than working a feather (slightly exaggerated, but not much). It is simple, it is easy, and it conserves a lot of energy.

You reach out and draw back toward the stern and, again let me emphasize, parallel to the keel. When the paddle is even with the hip, you feather it into rudder position by snapping your wrists up. Use your lower hand as the pivot point and you can steer with your forward hand. When you're on the right point (the direction you want to go), you pull out, reach forward and pull again. This stroke is not tiring and is particularly good when running white water because your paddle can easily be drawn back to the start of the stroke by feathering it through the water. This way it is always available for quick stops, correction, and bracing.

Several varieties of sweep strokes are often employed to turn a canoe. Some of them, while effective, consume a lot of energy. A typical sweep is executed by reaching forward and out, and then sweeping back in a wide arch where the blade is extended out into the water with the shaft at about a 45-degree angle from the water to the canoe. This maneuver, executed by both the bow and stern men on the same side, will turn the canoe in a wide circle. A variation of this can also be used to pivot the canoe within its own length. To perform this maneuver the bow man does a reverse sweep (just the reverse action of the above). On the opposite side of the canoe, the stern man employs a forward sweep. With a little practice, you can pivot your canoe around smartly.

To stop or brake a canoe, the following method works quite well. Simply thrust the paddle into the water at right angles to the keel and hold it steady against the gunwale. You may even be able to get a grip on the gunwale with your thumb. The shaft or loom should be straight up and down. This is a procedure that you must be able to execute quickly on the river, and although we will discuss this action and variations of it later on in the section on white water, it is important, I think, to mention here how it becomes a vital part of your training for the river.

When running the river, you may find it necessary to choose a new channel or avoid an obstruction as you make your way downstream. Since the canoe is traveling faster than water, you must first brake it and then paddle backward, angling the stern of the canoe slightly off the flow in the direction you wish to go. The flow of the water against the hull and your backpaddling will move the canoe over. This maneuver is called "setting." Later on we will discuss eddies, eddy walls, and other factors that play a part in this maneuver along with flow.

The accompanying illustration is typical of situations you often run into on the river. Your first impulse is to paddle with the main stream. If you spot the hazard in time, you may make the first bend, but the chances are not very good that you

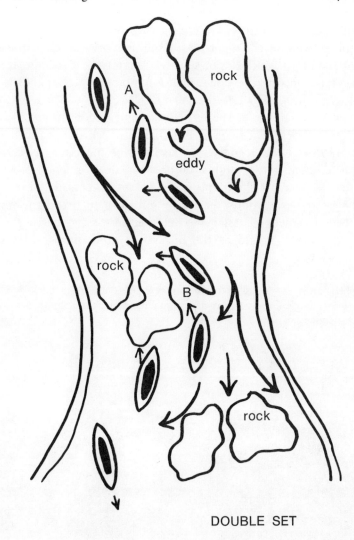

DOUBLE SET

would make the second turn. This we should refer to as a double set. By braking at point A and then backpaddling, be careful to align your canoe so that it will set to the right. Keep up the action until you are clear to proceed forward. Through this portion of the maneuver, I find it works better if the stern man paddles on the right side, assuming the set is right. It gives better control. As you approach point B, the paddlers can switch sides and angle the stern of the canoe toward the left so that you can set to the left. Brake and paddle in reverse until you are clear once again, and then proceed down the river.

It does take strength to execute this maneuver effectively, so practice it thoroughly before you need it. Remember also that you are pushing the water in the direction it is flowing so your strokes must be swift and deep in order to establish the movement necessary to set you across the current.

Setting is as old as the hills. It is used often when white

This craft is propelled by water power as it ferries back and forth across the Rhine at the end of a pulley and cable rig in Basel, Switzerland.

water canoeing. It is used when poling both upstream and down. Extended sets, going from one side of the river to the other, is called ferrying. A small token from the "for what it's worth department" shows how the current is used in a more sophisticated manner on such rivers as the Rhine. For centuries, the current has pushed motorless boats back and forth across the river in such places as Basel, Switzerland. Behind the cathedral is a long cable stretched to the far shore high above the river. Another cable riding on a pulley is attached to a small pedestrian ferry boat that, when properly set to the current, runs back and forth smartly, as it has on this river for centuries.

While still on the subject of paddling—and to make it clear just what is happening with the water in the river during the various strokes—I will mention standing waves, haystacks, eddies, and eddy walls. I will talk about them in great detail later, but for now it is a good idea to understand what they are.

The standing wave is just what you would expect it to be, a wave that doesn't move. They vary in size according to the flow of the river and are found in the deepest part of the channel. Beyond the standing waves you often find haystacks, white piles of loose water, usually caused by fast moving water running into slow water. They are harmless except that they can get you very wet and cause you a lot of bailing. An eddy is the place to go if you want to get away from it all. It can be used to rest, a sort of oasis or mid-river parking lot. They are caused by back currents and are found behind rocks. The eddy wall is the obstacle you have to cross to get into the eddy. It is caused by fast water rubbing against slow-water currents going in the opposite direction. Water here is usually flowing in two different directions and therefore can flip you around or even roll your canoe over.

The accompanying illustration shows the river being squeezed together by the obstructions along the banks. The deepest water is revealed by the standing waves. As the river

Couple rides over a set of standing waves as they make their way
down river.

Canoers charge through turbulent water (haystacks) caused by obstructions and swift water pushing into slower water. Canoe would
have stayed a lot drier had the bow paddler positioned herself further
aft before arriving at this obstacle on the river.

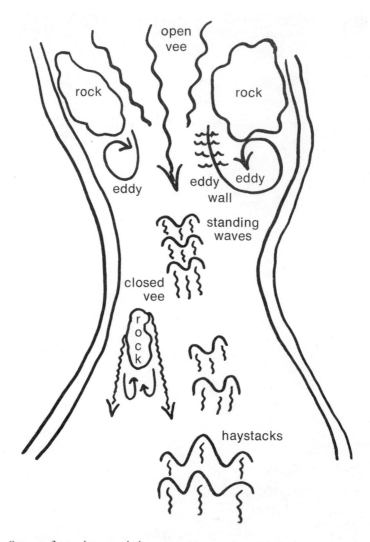

Stream-flow characteristics.

opens up again, the current runs into slower water causing haystacks. Behind the rocks are the eddies. As indicated by the
arrows, the currents work backward to fill the area behind the
rocks with water. The eddy wall is a narrow ridge of small
turbulent waves that is the result of slow water moving back

upstream against the rushing flow of the current downstream.

To give a clearer description of the various maneuvers and paddle strokes used in canoeing, I will take some time here to further define them, illustrate them, and describe how they are used.

SPLIT DRAW ˅

The split draw is used to move the canoe forward. By adjusting the amount of pull, each paddler can quickly determine what he must do to keep the canoe moving forward. Care should be given to be sure the draw runs parallel with the keel and that the blade remains at right angles to the keel.

J DRAW

This stroke is somewhat useful for keeping the bow up to the point in a crosswind and for turning. The blade at the end of the draw is curved out as in a J. The stroke is usually performed by the stern man.

FEATHER DRAW GLIDE ˋ

Actually there are several names given to this stroke. I call it the feather draw glide because it reminds me of all that is happening in each stroke. Yet it is easy to perform and provides maximum control over your canoe without causing a drag. As in the strokes already mentioned, you reach forward and pull the blade back parallel with the keel. When the blade is even with your side, you feather it with a flick of the hand and a twist of the wrist either clockwise or counterclockwise. This places the blade in line or parallel with the keel. Let it angle back a bit and then, by shifting the blade to the

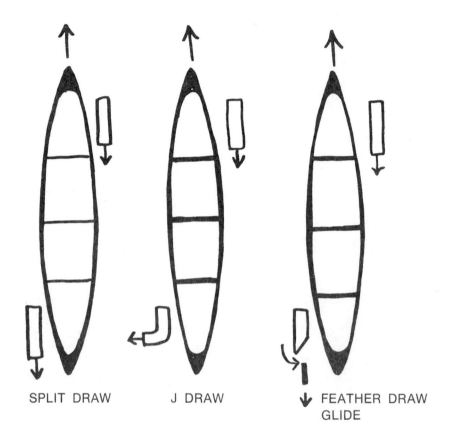

SPLIT DRAW   J DRAW   FEATHER DRAW
                                    GLIDE

left or to the right, your paddle serves as a rudder. This stroke is normally executed by the stern man while the bow man continues his regular draw.

BRAKE

This is used to stop the canoe. The paddle is placed in the water at right angles to the keel. If you wish to slide over as you brake, you can angle the leading edge of the blade in the

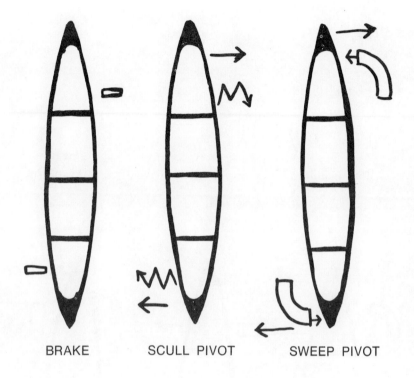

BRAKE   SCULL PIVOT   SWEEP PIVOT

direction you wish to go. Hold the paddle shaft as straight and rigid as you can.

SCULL PIVOT

For pivoting or moving over. Place the paddle in the water at about a 45-degree angle to the keel. The shaft should be perpendicular. Allow yourself some room in the water and, with a sculling action, moving the blade alternately through the water with a flick of the wrist, draw the canoe toward the paddle.

SWEEP PIVOT

In this pivot, the shaft here is extended out from the canoe and swept in an arch.

SWEEP TURN

Both paddlers sweep on the left to make a gradual right turn.

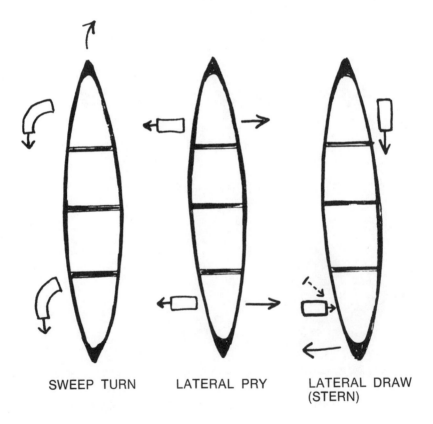

SWEEP TURN   LATERAL PRY   LATERAL DRAW (STERN)

LATERAL PRY

This maneuver, which can be executed by both paddlers, either together or independently, is used to move over quickly in a stream. Brace your paddle against the gunwale and pry with your upper hand. Use caution here unless you know the paddle handle can take the strain. Never try this with a spruce paddle and go tenderly with ash. This maneuver works best with a canoe that has a shoe keel or no keel at all.

LATERAL DRAW

Used to pull the stern canoe over a notch, the draw can be executed by either paddler or both. It may be done at a 90-degree angle, as shown in the diagram, or a 45-degree angle, as indicated by the dotted line. It takes teamwork and practice to execute this one properly when making a sharp turn into a swiftly moving current.

PUSH

The push can be used by either or both paddlers. Again, take care with this one. It is used like the pry, to slide the canoe over, and I like it better. The difference is that the lower hand moves out and away from the gunwale with the paddle, keeping the shaft alignment somewhat perpendicular or angled forward.

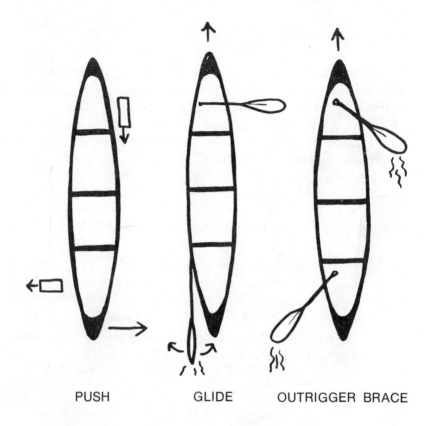

PUSH   GLIDE   OUTRIGGER BRACE

GLIDE

Just a restful way to enjoy the passing landscape and maintain control over your canoe with no more than an occasional sweep or draw.

OUTRIGGER BRACE

This can be very useful in a wide, fast moving river where the water is white and the eddy walls are snapping away on

one side and haystacks on the other. In runs where there is great turbulence and the course is straight ahead, it makes for a leveler and more stable ride. The paddles can quickly be summoned to action also. In an emergency, if you are capsizing, you can thrust down hard on the water from this position and check the roll. This sort of maneuver is often referred to as a low brace, because what you are actually doing is bracing yourself and the canoe by holding the paddle against the water. In a sense, it performs the function of an outrigger, which is why I refer to this paddle action as an outrigger brace.

The methods just mentioned will take care of getting your canoe safely downriver with a minimum of confusion. However, there are several other useful maneuvers and variations. One of them is the *bow rudder*. This is a physically demanding technique that requires strong arms. In executing the bow rudder it is possible to get poked in the face with the handle of the paddle or even to end up in the drink. For these reasons, I really have reservations about the technique. However, if you've seen others doing it and want to give it a try, here's how it works.

The bow man extends the blade of his paddle out into the water at about a 45-degree angle to the canoe, leaning forward to achieve good balance. His upper hand should be close to his chest so he doesn't end up with the handle in his mouth or neck. His lower hand should be extended down the shaft toward the throat and with muscles poised and body braced, he takes his position and holds while the stern man reverse sweeps on the same side or executes some other maneuver that will swing the stern around.

There are occasions when the bow man may wish to cross over with his paddle without changing hands so that he can execute a quick draw stroke. This is an acceptable maneuver and is more powerful than a pry from the paddler's regular side. What's more, it is much less risky if done in shallow water where a pry, if the paddle wedges in a rock, could upset the canoe. This stroke is referred to as a *cross draw* and is very effective if executed properly. Strong leg leverage against the hull is necessary when executing this stroke because the body is twisted and knee support is essential to maintain balance.

4

Progress Without a Paddle: *Poling, Snubbing, Portage, Lining, Double-Lining*

Poling

IF YOU RUN OUT OF PADDLES you can always use a pole. As a matter of fact, poling, when properly performed, is one of the finer arts of canoeing. When poling you must, of course, stand up. You take a position in the stern of the canoe so that the bow is just slightly raised, then, keeping the pole close to the gunwale with your feet apart at about a 45-degree angle with the keel, push against the bottom and work your way hand-over-hand up the pole. At the end, gently flex the knees and thrust forward with a final shove. Retrieve the pole hand-over-hand and start the motion over. A sapling about 14 feet long is

Poling upstream using 14-foot sapling with metal shoe on bottom of pole to prevent slipping and hold the pole to the riverbed.

a good choice, unless you are interested in purchasing an aluminum one. To pole with ease and not have it slip on the bottom, your pole should have a metal shoe. Poling does require a bit of practice, but when you get the hang of it, you can go upstream or down with a few basic techniques.

Snubbing

A method known as snubbing is a simple technique for changing the direction of the bow. You hold, or snub, the canoe with the pole, and the water will move the bow over toward the direction you want to go. When it is where you want it, ship the pole, set it, and begin your forward motion. Of course, this method of locomotion is for shallow streams, not rivers with rushing white water. Once you learn how to snub, it can be a lot of fun and is great for exploring small, out-of-the-way streams where a paddle would be virtually useless.

Portage

For transporting a canoe on land, the simplest and most popular method is portage. The dictionary defines portage as "the carrying of boats and goods overland between navigable bodies of water."

For the ultimate in portaging comfort, you can invest in a set of yokes with soft shoulder cushions. They are fine if you plan to do a lot of portaging over great distances, but for an occasional carry of a few hundred yards or so, paddles will do just fine.

If you decide to use your paddles, have your partner place them on your shoulders in order to get some idea of how far you want the blades of the paddle to be apart so that you can fit your head in the yoke and have the blades near the throat rest on your shoulder. You would be surprised how often people overestimate the width of their shoulders, and when they toss the canoe up into the air the first time they go right through the yoke and bang their head on the bottom. An old guide friend of mine on Long Pond up on Mt. Desert Island, Maine, used to call this "ringing the bell."

When you figure what the right separation is for you, place the paddles in a vee between the middle thwart and the bow thwart. The handles should be toward the bow so that your shoulders will carry the blades just behind the throat of the paddle close to the center thwart. Secure the paddles well so that they will not shift when you toss the canoe into the air.

Then, if the position is correct, mark it on the thwarts. I always place my sweater over my shoulder and tie it in the front. If the paddles are spaced correctly and your sweater is in place, you will be quite amazed at how comfortable that canoe will feel up there.

Actually preparing your canoe for portage and lifting it onto your shoulders sounds far more difficult than it is. However, the river bank on the morning of departure is no time to try this one for the first time. After you get your body in

To make a long portage more comfortable you can make a yoke out of your paddles. I tie the blades together as shown to prevent slippage. The life jacket with the neck rest makes a great supporting pad for a portage.

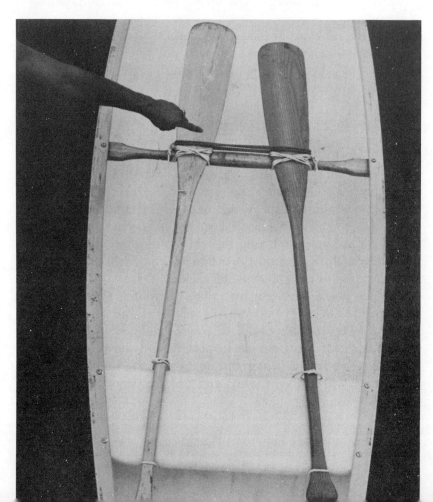

shape early in the spring, practice it in the backyard with a friend, preferably one who has already mastered the technique.

Stop-motion photography is used here to show how to lift a canoe for portage. It is really quite easy, provided all your muscles are doing what they are supposed to be doing at the proper time. My good friend and white water canoeing enthusiast, Ned Lutz, tosses this Old Town up on his shoulders with ease.

The secret is in the initial grip and thrust. Both hands must grip the thwart with the palms facing forward or the direction in which you plan to face. Motion is started by a coordinated push with the knees and pull of the thwart.

Free of the knees the arms continue to lift and the legs and body begin to straighten.

The body continues to straighten and the weight is gradually shifted to the left foot. The canoe continues to rise as the arms continue to lift.

At this point most of the weight is on the left foot making it possible to begin swinging the right foot around about 90 degrees to the right.

At this point the canoe has reached maximum height. The right leg and body continue to pivot to the right.

The left arm pushes as the right arm eases the canoe into portage position.

The body now has moved completely to the right, about 90 degrees, and the canoe is in place.

With the canoe squarely balanced on the shoulders, the hands can now be extended along the gunwale for better balance and control.

The two-man lift works exactly the same way as the single-man lift. The palms all must face in the direction of the portage.

The knee flip sends the canoe on its way.

Up and over.

Ready on top. This method is good for two people storing canoes on racks or on top of cars. Handled by two people, there is less chance of bumping up the car.

Setting the canoe down again is the exact reverse of this procedure. When you try raising and lowering your canoe for the first time, it is best to have your experienced friend guide one end of the canoe and coach you and be there like a spotter just in case your timing is off. The important things here are timing and that all-important push with the knee followed by the swing. If everyone goes together, you will feel like a champion weightlifter. But be careful, if there are a lot of people around the launch site, lower the canoe from the portage position early and walk the canoe to the water with your partner. This precludes the possibility of banging some innocent bystander in the head if for some reason you turn around a bit.

There are other techniques for raising a canoe for portage, but most of them require more effort or additional equipment. The procedure mentioned above is applicable for just about all canoes.

Lining

There are situations you may run into in the future where the only way to go up or down the river with your canoe will

Two men can also carry the canoe as illustrated here.

be by lining, moving the boat along with ropes or "lines." The advantage of lining over portage is that you may not have to unload your canoe. Still, you must know what you are doing in order to keep your canoe from ramming into the bank or getting snagged.

If two men can't handle it, you can always use four.

In order for lining to be executed with snap and precision, certain prerequisites must be provided by nature. First of all, the river should be of gentle to moderate flow. Never try to line a canoe on a swift river, unless there is no other alternative. Secondly, the river should be relatively free of stones and other obstacles that could get in the way of your lines. Finally, there should be no overhanging bushes along the banks.

As you can well imagine, the areas where you might want to line do not always have the prerequisites, so a portage is often more practical. Likewise, however, there are also situations where a portage around an obstacle, upstream or down, is impossible, and your only alternative is lining. For instance, a sudden change in flow characteristics turns what is normally a passable hazard into a raging torrent. High cliffs on either side of the river prohibit a portage. Lining is your only way out.

Before you plunge into this, however, there are a few things you had better check out first, unless you want to be left behind without a canoe. Be sure that you can climb along the

This method of lining a canoe through hazardous ledges can be performed upstream or down. In either case, care should be taken to keep the canoe in line with the stream flow so that it does not broach.

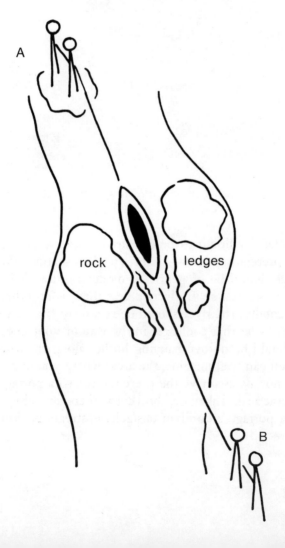

edge of the river and find a place, preferably an accessible eddy below the hazard, where you can reclaim your canoe. In doing this, you may find a way of walking it around through shallows that would save you what could become an engineering feat.

If possible, let the canoe down on a single line from a position of vantage, preferably in line with passage. All persons must lend a hand here, both at the starting point and the finish. Remember, also, the safety of the two or more people you may need to lower the canoe through the hazard. Be sure you have safety lines to them held by others in the party. Take only one canoe at a time and be sure it is empty if the river is mean. The line should be fastened low under the bow to prevent yawing (moving from side to side). A second line should also be attached and that one hand carried down to the team that will retrieve the canoe from the current. Make sure you have plenty of muscle power here in case the craft capsizes or fills with water. Also, find a convenient rock that you can snub the line around if you have to. As the canoe is lowered, the downriver team should take up the slack but both teams must be alert to the effects of the currents on the canoe. It might be better at times to let it go swiftly or to hold it back. Whatever the case, both teams should keep taut lines to minimize danger of snagging.

After the obstruction or hazard is negotiated, the downriver team, using their line, can move the craft into the eddy. They can then secure the canoe, return their line and start on the next canoe. This is an example of the exception rather than the rule, but nevertheless it is good to know how to line downstream but I hope you won't have to use it.

Double-Lining

Double-lining on a barge canal can be a very pleasant experience by contrast. Here, a line is placed on both the bow

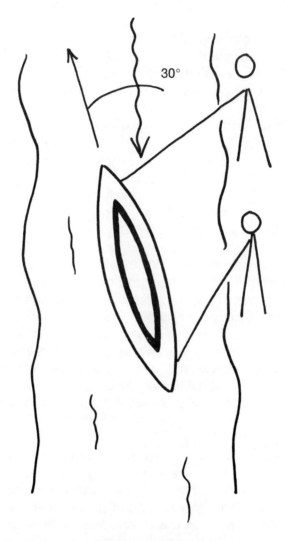

30°

When double-lining a canoe upstream in this manner, it is necessary to haul it at about a 30-degree angle to the stream flow. This prevents it from yawing and running into the bank.

and the stern. The stern man walks the same path as the bow man and, in relation to the canoe, is in a position abeam. To keep the canoe under control, it is slipped up the river at about a 30-degree angle to the current. The bow man must provide enough line so that his end of the canoe, the bow, will ride over across the current. When the proper positioning is achieved, both men walk up the river holding the lines and keeping the correct distance from one another so that the attitude of the canoe to the current remains the same.

It is possible, but not practical, to negotiate this maneuver with one line attached to a bridle extending from the bow to the center thwart. The line is attached to the bridle so that the canoe will pull with its bow angled from the shore. Care must be taken here that the line does not fall slack. The pull must be steady and the river gentle.

If your canoe is not equipped with fittings on the bow and stern, a bridle can easily be made for any of the above operations or for towing behind another boat. Run a line from the front of the bow seat next to the gunwale under the canoe to the same position on the other side. Leave a little slack and attach another line to the middle of the loop under the canoe in line with the keel. The pull should be from underneath, close to the bow to prevent yawing.

5

Reading the River

On most rivers where canoeing is popular, it is possible to obtain, through local or national canoe organizations or state or county commissions, maps and/or charts of the rivers which show campsites, launch areas, channel depths, and stream-flow characteristics. Rivers in the East (and I specify East because I have always felt that the Western rivers are tougher) classified from Grade 0 for a placid pool up to Grade 6 for hazardous rapids. Westerners quite modestly point out, however, that though Western rivers may have higher waves, said waves are farther apart and therefore easier to ride. In any case, these ratings are important and should not be taken lightly. You should be careful not to canoe beyond your ability because the ways of the river can be swift, subtle, and sometimes cruel.

As an illustration of how serious the situation can become, let me relate a terrifying experience several young friends of

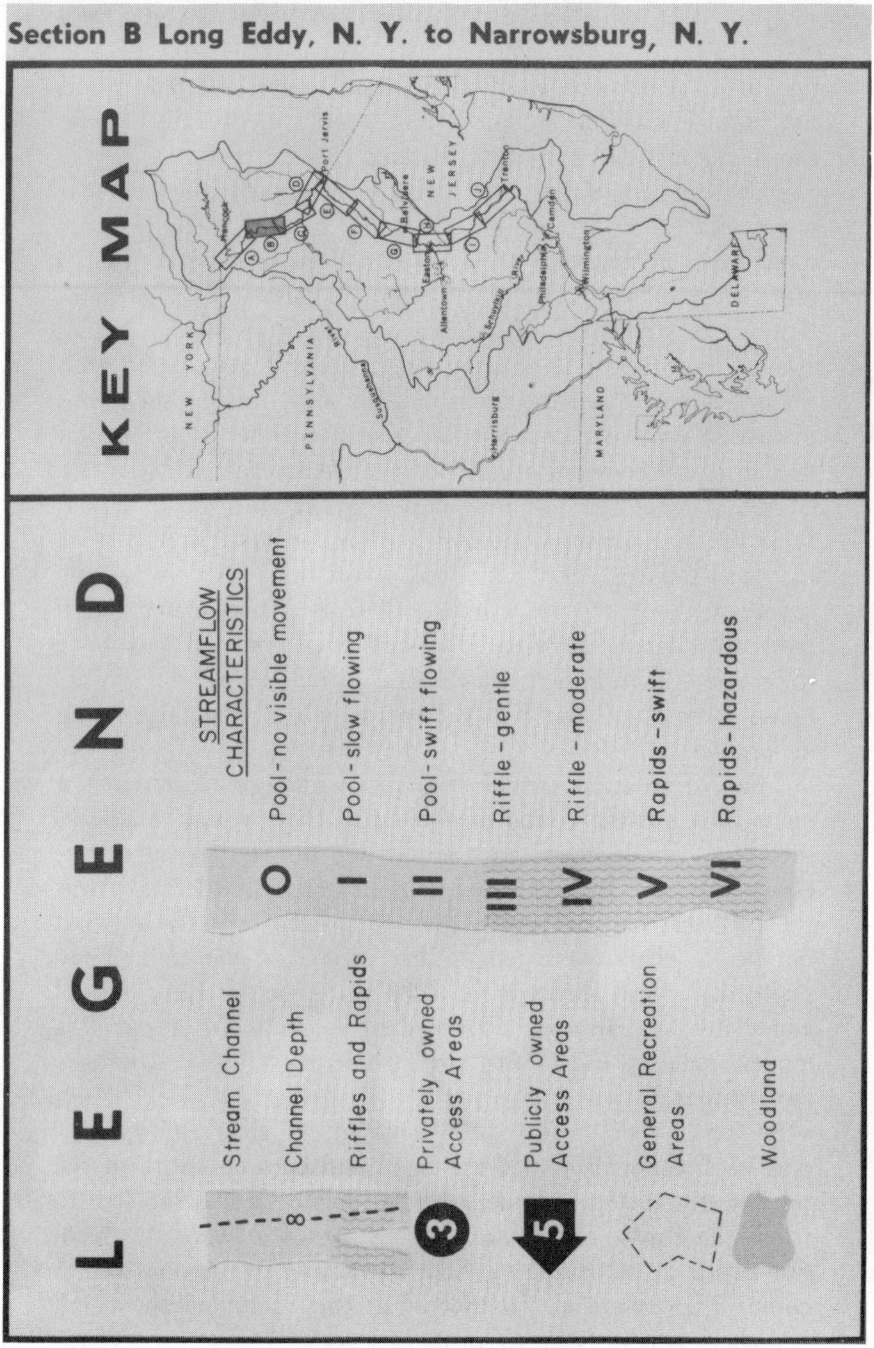
Section B Long Eddy, N. Y. to Narrowsburg, N. Y.
LEGEND
Stream Channel
8
Channel Depth
Riffles and Rapids
3
Privately owned Access Areas
5
Publicly owned Access Areas
General Recreation Areas
Woodland
STREAMFLOW CHARACTERISTICS
O
Pool - no visible movement
I
Pool - slow flowing
II
Pool - swift flowing
III
Riffle - gentle
IV
Riffle - moderate
V
Rapids - swift
VI
Rapids - hazardous
KEY MAP
NEW YORK
PENNSYLVANIA
NEW JERSEY
MARYLAND
DELAWARE
Hancock
Port Jervis
Belvidere
Easton
Allentown
Trenton
Philadelphia
Camden
Wilmington
Harrisburg
Susquehanna River
Schuylkill River

Legend and map of the Delaware River, typical of material available through state and local agencies.

mine had because they used poor judgment and allowed that all too familiar attitude among young people to prevail, "I'll be careful, don't worry, it won't happen to me."

Last year four young men, who were good whitewater canoers, elected to explore an unfamiliar section of the Housatonic River in Connecticut. They left home in the early morning with two kayaks and two small open canoes. Their destination was a stretch of river that included Bulls Bridge below Kent, Connecticut. The young men were well acquainted with the upper portion of the river and, for some reason, felt it was unnecessary to check out the lower section either by inspection or inquiry. They had a copy of the "Appalachian Mountain Club Canoeing Guide" and simply ignored its recommendations for a shore inspection of the area around Bulls Bridge that was rated 4. The guidebook states that, "About ¼ mile before reaching the powerhouse, there is a particularly rough pitch which may have to be looked over first and may have to be lined down in high water. And ½ mile below the powerhouse there is another heavy pitch which may require lining in high water."

This information should have been enough to initiate an inspection, but the young men felt that they would be able to spot any trouble ahead and would pull out if it became necessary. What they neglected to take into consideration was the fact that the river was low and instead of a fast-moving number 4, there were ledges that created a waterfall. They proceeded ahead through the deep water below Kent School and eventually approached the dam area moving ahead at a modest pace in Indian file, the two kayaks followed by the two canoes.

Suddenly there was a sharp bend in the river and, one by one, each canoer rounded the bend and became aware of the terrible mistake in judgment he had made. It was too late to reach the bank. The roar that they had not heard upstream now made it impossible to shout a warning to the ones yet to come. They were all committed as they rounded the bend, and there was no way to escape.

The first kayak disappeared over the falls just as the second kayak realized he had no choice but to follow. The same was true of the canoes. As the first kayak plunged over the falls, it miraculously escaped plunging into the rocks and instead slammed bow first into a small pool of water, but shattered as it was split open on the rocks below. The pilot of the ill-fated craft was somehow thrown clear and, after being battered against the rocks by the terrible force of the water, managed to crawl to safety on a large boulder just in time to see his terrified companion in the second kayak follow nearly the same line. Realizing the two canoes were somewhere above, Dave tried desperately to shout above the roar of the water, but he could barely hear his own voice, the sound of the crushing water was so intense. He could not even hear the crash of Paul's kayak as it plunged into the froth which concealed the rocks.

For a moment there was nothing. The river seemed to have swallowed Paul as well as the kayak until, rising like a serpent from the deep in agonizing disarray, the kayak shot into the air, flipped backward and was slammed broadside on the rocks. This final agonizing crash could be heard above the roar of the river and then, once again, there was nothing except a few small pieces of blue fiberglass that raced off as the craft was thrown clear of the churning waters under the falls. Dave was frantic. Where was Paul? His eyes scanned wildly back and forth across the river. Where was he, where was Paul? Dave thought for sure his companion had been carried downstream or pinned under a rock.

Suddenly Barry appeared at the lip of the falls in the first canoe. He had evidently seen Paul's plunge in time to signal Frank, who was behind him. As he started over the edge, he was still waving frantically. As the bow dropped over, Barry turned in time to see what was before him. He plunged feet first with his paddle clutched in both hands. Not more than six inches separated him from the canoe. The stern of the canoe began to pitch forward just as Barry entered the water in a tremendous splash. Dave hoped Barry would be deep enough

Single paddler entering turbulent section of the New Haven River near Bristol, Vermont.

so that he would not be hit by the canoe as it crashed in on top of him.

Suddenly Dave noticed a black blob rising from the water. It was hair. As it came to the surface, there was Paul given up by the water, regurgitated by the falls. His eyes were bugged as he gasped for breath and crawled for the base of the huge rock near Dave. As Dave crawled over to give Paul a hand,

Flow pattern of water over the rocks causes a foamy eddy from a looping action which mixes it with air. This is often called a haystack.

he felt the sticky feeling of blood in his shoes which were catching the run-off from two nasty gashes on each ankle. With much effort, he pulled Paul out of the water and both young men stretched out across the cold stone gasping and choking for air. Paul's deck shoes had been ripped from his feet and his life jacket had been slashed as if by a knife.

As Dave looked toward the river again he could see Barry, his head above the water and still clutching his paddle. Somehow his glasses were still in place. He had landed differently than Paul and Dave and because of that was carried downstream about 25 yards before he was able to pull himself out.

Paul turned his head and looked toward the falls. Dave and Barry waved to each other, glad they were both alive. All eyes were now on the lip of the falls waiting for Frank.

Over on another large rock by a large pool further in toward the right bank of the river was a fisherman. Through all of this he had stood transfixed like a statue unable to move. Suddenly, so it seemed, his favorite fishing hole had been invaded. It had become choked with crushed debris and struggling bodies. He stood there, still unable to move.

Finally Frank appeared. You could see as he approached the lip how he frantically searched for the right place to drop. He sprang out in the direction of the deep part of the river, his legs and arms pumping as if he were trying to run forward. His canoe began to roll as it fell and it got caught by the falling water. It was driven hard into the bottom of the river. It rolled and pitched and finally was spun out to the side where its now battered hulk was wedged between the rocks not far from the fisherman's pool. The fisherman now raised his arm and feebly gestured toward the falls. Frank had been thrown back under the falls and was being pounded by the tons of water that came crushing down upon him. It was almost inconceivable that he could possibly survive the angry battering he was receiving. Suddenly, like the canoe, he was tossed out for an instant. He looked desperate as he reached out, grasping for anything that would pull him from the angry grip of the falls.

Suddenly he sank, rolling over and over, and disappeared from sight in the turbulent water. Exhausted Paul and Dave lay on the rock helpless. Barry could hardly comprehend what was happening. It was almost a full minute since Frank had plunged over the lip and the boys thought for sure that the river had claimed its victim. It was as if it had sampled each one of them and had finally selected the one it wanted.

Just as everyone was beginning to give Frank up, he suddenly popped to the surface directly in front of the fisherman who finally had reeled in his line. He gasped for air and then proceeded to get sick. The fisherman still did not seem able to accept what was happening in his fishing hole. As Frank managed to pull his battered body up onto the fisherman's rock, the fisherman leaned over and offered him his hand. In a sort of reflex manner, he asked if he was all right and then quickly retreated toward his car.

It was a good five minutes before anyone moved. Barry finally managed to get across the river and together the four boys checked for broken bones. Much to their surprise, none of them was seriously injured. They had some pretty bad bruises and lacerations but most of the blood was from superficial scratches. They had all survived. They were lucky to be alive. One kayak and one canoe were totally destroyed, another kayak was damaged almost beyond repair, and the second aluminum canoe looked as if it had been run over by a trailer truck.

Once you commit yourself to a stretch of rapids, there is no turning back, and it can be difficult to stop. You must move with the water. As exhilarating and enjoyable as whitewater canoeing is, it is often dangerous, and you must be constantly on the alert for what lies ahead of you.

Before attempting white water yourself, go with someone who has had experience, or join a local club. Take along a guide, and be sure you are in good shape physically and mentally. Know what you are doing, where you are going, and how, if necessary, to handle an emergency. Never go alone and never go on a trip where there are less than three canoes or six people. Never travel at night.

The situation is improving, but there are still canoe rental places where they will not even bother to ask you about your experience. They may give you an extra paddle and probably a life jacket, but they will not insist that you wear it. They will insist that you leave a deposit and sign a paper absolving the outfitter of any responsibility and requiring you to make good for any damages you inflict on his canoe. This latter part is quite proper, but I still yearn for the day when a canoer is checked out more carefully before being turned loose on the

river. It is unfortunate that we bring federal or state controls
down upon ourselves in such recreational areas as this, but
there seems to be no alternative. The park service already has
many constraints against paddle boats on the Grand Canyon
and is in the process of getting new ones approved. Renting
a canoe for the river is a far cry from renting one to take a
spin around the park. So learn how to read the river and detect
its warnings before you run it.

Most stream-flow characteristics are obtained and most
streams are rated during a period of low-flow conditions, so
it must be remembered that these are minimum values. In the
springtime or in very short order following a rainstorm or the
opening of a dam upstream, a number 3 hazard could take on
the characteristics of a number 5. It also should be taken into
account that water level can cover up hazards making them
passable without difficulty, or it can reveal them too late and
cause serious difficulties if you do not read the warning signs
correctly. Try to follow the channel on the map. Follow es-
sentially the outside of the curve, and remember, what might
be a fast-moving number 5 today at high water could, by next
week, become a treacherous rock shelf if the water were lower.

The presence of ledges or a sudden drop in the river is revealed upstream by the appearance of a smooth line across that
portion of the river. Remember the importance of this sign
when on the river. It is like a red flashing light. The river line
is often accompanied by a warning roar from the turbulent
waters below. But that line across the river is always a dead
giveaway of either rapids, ledges, or a waterfall. If you cannot
determine what is beyond that line by standing up in the canoe,
then you should immediately head for shore and proceed on
foot to determine what's ahead. Do not wait too long. The
closer you get to the edge of the line, the faster the river will
be flowing, and if you wait too long and you're in the middle
of the river, you may not have enough time to escape before
being swept over the ledges or falls.

If you find yourself committed to running a ledge or water-

It is important to check the water level of the river and know precisely the effects of a drop in water level where ledges exist. Ignoring water level could result in a situation like this.

fall, try to pick the spot where the most water is running, for two reasons. The first obvious one is to prevent getting hung up on the lip, and the other one, less obvious, is to provide yourself with a better passage out of the area after the drop. If there is a drop of several feet, you are bound to run into what is often called a white eddy. This is where the surface water rolls back toward where the water is spilling over. It can be dangerous, especially if there is a large roller wave created by this situation. It could bring you to a screeching

These two river runners have just dropped off the edge of the river and are probably wondering what happened to their canoe. The straight, even line across the lower portion of the picture stands out distinctly from upstream. From above, the turbulence would not be visible. The line unmistakably indicates a sharp drop or even dam. It is a signal to anyone not familiar with the area to pull toward shore and check out the river from land before proceeding.

halt and the action of the back water on the surface versus the forward movement of the water underneath could cause you to broach or roll over. When you go over the lip in this situation, pull hard and deep. This will keep the canoe driving forward. If you try to stop on the lip as I have seen some people do, you will almost certainly capsize, or get your bow

Water pattern indicates quite vividly the presence of a ledge. With care, it can be navigated by following the chute just beyond the rock in the foreground or, more conservatively, by following the vees toward the left of the picture.

buried to the point where you will swamp. If you see it coming in time, the bow man, if he is quick, can kneel behind his seat to keep the bow up, but what is really important is to keep the bow driving forward and straight, and pull your paddles deep so that you get a bite on the solid water moving forward under the surface turbulence.

Water flow can accurately reflect the condition of the river bottom. When the river is running moderate and smooth, a small disturbance on the surface is an indication of a deep rock. No problem here. If, however, the river is running *slowly* there may not be any indication and because the water level would be down if such were the case, the rock could be just

Turbulence caused by rock deflecting the flow of water. You must be able to determine how far above the turbulence the rock is situated. Depth and stream flow are factors here.

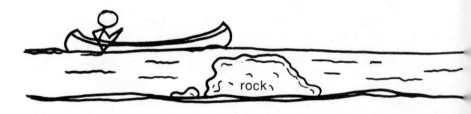

In very slow moving water there may be no indication of rock.

under the surface. Flat rocks, just below the surface, can appear almost as smooth-crowned bumps on the upriver side. Below the rock, however, will be a disturbance. Watch out for these revealing signs, and avoid such hazards.

As the water flows between protruding rocks it forms a vee, showing the passage. The center of the vee, or where it comes together, usually has a few standing waves whose size is determined by the depth and flow. This comparatively tranquil vee

These canoers making their way through the rocks will not be fooled by the smooth, dark bump in the foreground. The clue here is the bump, and the smoothness is a dead giveaway that there is something just under the surface.

is usually the safest route for you to follow through the white water.

Also keep in mind that the swiftness of the river determines

Canoers guide their canoe into the open vee through the rocks and past the fallen tree.

the distance between obstructions and where they show themselves on the surface. The faster the flow, the further upstream away from the sign is where the rock will be. Learn these signs and learn them well.

After passage over rock or ledges the looping action of the water often creates turbulence accompanied by a wave as seen here.

Pot holes such as this are often found just under the surface on fast moving rivers. They can be a hazard if your feet or legs become caught in them. Keep this in mind should you decide to get out of your canoe.

As you approach an island in the river you might assume that the best route forward is straight ahead. The river may even appear wider than the branch which goes off to the side. You must be quick to size up the situation here. You must determine, by reading the water, whether you have enough depth on the straight stretch forward. If the water is high you may be okay, but the chances are that the main course of the river is the one that bends around the island. It may be narrower, but a quick look at the banks and the island will pretty much tell you that the straight-ahead course is the result of flood erosion caused by increased run-off upstream. Unless the river is running full, the chances are the passage will be shallow and troublesome.

Islands caused by erosion are increasingly common in areas where there has been excessive lumbering or population

In hot pursuit of the guy who pulled the plug out of the river.

growth. A single tree absorbs, on the average, over 100 gallons of water each day and when entire forests are cleared
away, the run-off can be increased by billions of gallons a day.
The run-off contains silt and topsoil and can change the characteristics of river flow dramatically. Watch for evidence of
this and study all the signs before committing yourself to the
passage. Always take the deepest route; chances are it will be
the main channel and the safest.

6

Navigating White Water

It can be said that whitewater canoeing is like threading your way down a steep mountain trail on skis. You must constantly change course, check, and traverse, and all the while you must be thinking ahead, concentrating on the turns and moguls or standing waves and haystacks. With whitewater canoeing, however, there is one major difference: The surface is moving as well as you, and not necessarily in a single downhill direction. It is a whole new dimension you are dealing with. There are ferocious little crosscurrents that reach out and grab at your canoe, and it is difficult to stop once you are committed. Picture yourself on a steep moguled trail that suddenly springs into motion. All of a sudden the entire covering of snow begins to move swiftly downhill, jumping and rolling over the bumps and crevasses. If you can imagine yourself

Sliding down the river is similar to skiing down a trail.

skiing on this moving mass, then you have some idea of what it is like to thread your way down a swiftly moving river.

In this section I will try to present what I feel is important to know about running a river in an open canoe. The purpose here is to present enough information so that you will clearly understand how to deal with the currents, the eddies, and the various forces of water that sometimes are with you and at other times are against you. I will share with you some personal experiences and anecdotes which I hope will better illustrate this great experience of whitewater canoeing and camping in an open canoe. It is not meant to be a handbook for slalom and racing techniques on the river, but what is discussed here can certainly be applied and serve as a background to these specialties.

Riding the rapids or white water is truly one of the greatest thrills of canoeing. A rapid is a swift flow of water where rocks and the pitch of the river cause turbulence. They are like large bumps on a washboard road or, as some like to refer to them, steps on a river.

River flow, as we mentioned earlier, is rated 0 to 6. Zero is the rating given to a quiet pool where there is no noticeable river flow. You would want to paddle through an area rated 0, normally a deep pool in a wide part of the river. Canoeing through a number 1 rapid, you become aware of movement, and if you can see the bottom, you notice that it is slipping behind you. On number 2, you begin to feel the movement of the water and notice small, white ripples forward of the protruding rocks. The river seems alive because you notice it gurgling. Riding through the number 3, you realize that the river is running downhill. Its jovial gurgle begins to really sound like rushing water determined on going somewhere. The canoe starts to bob and you begin to move as fast as you do when you paddle swiftly. Your paddles move effortlessly through the draw, and the canoe flows faster than the water. The number 4 water begins to roar. You suddenly become aware that your canoe moves at a fast pace past rocks and ledges. It, too, springs to life. The shoreline moves behind quickly, and you learn fast that the river demands full concentration, that the corrections you make in your course have to be done well in advance of the obstructions.

Suddenly you look down and see a large boulder slip by just under the surface. The water above it is smooth and then you notice it is quite a few feet before the water begins to wrinkle with ribbons of white. You realize how far upstream the obstacle was from where it revealed itself. You are aware of how alert you must be, how you must read the river, how you must constantly look ahead for signs of obstructions and make your corrections in course as soon as possible.

All at once the air is filled with spray; you are in number 5s! You brace yourself again, moving your paddle quickly and straining to get a good bite on the water. You find your paddle must dip deep. Your canoe now feels like a wild stallion, lurching, diving, and dashing ahead. It lifts up onto the standing waves and then plunges down their backsides into reeling piles of white water. The sound is deafening. You have to yell loudly to your bow man. Large odd shapes which you recognize as blobs of water fly by the gunwales, twisting and turning and occasionally leaping into the craft. You and your bow man make a few correcting sweeps, your knees press heavily on your kneeling pad, and you can feel the water squish out. Your paddle bends and twists. The thought occurs in a flash. "Will it snap?" you say to yourself! Through the roar, you hear the rasping sound of agony as metal pits its strength against a solid mass of stone. You see the stone quickly slip by just under the seething water. "We made it, we made it!" you cry. The stone is behind you. You are racing along at a tremendous pace. You are concerned about your canoe, but as you feel it lifting and lunging, you know it is still very much alive. You marvel at the way it rides through the water. Its determination stands out with every movement. The roar gets deeper and louder.

You suddenly put your mind back to the river. You feel small and almost buried because now the standing waves are even with your shoulders as you continue to roll forward. Spray is all around. As you look downhill you see watery haystacks everywhere heaving and throbbing and tugging at the

Single paddler guides his canoe into position for his next passage through the rapids.

bottom. Approaching the open vees, you say, "Follow the vees!" Suddenly you crash into a haystack. All you can see is water. Your bow man is lost in the spray but he is still aboard as you come out of the frothy mass. The canoe continues to move forward, the river slows down up ahead, and once again you hear the cry of the crow and the far-off buzz of a chain saw in action. The roar of the river is far behind you now and it seems to have settled down for a rest. You made it down through the 5s, or were they running 6s! Dripping wet, you and your bow man bail out some water and wearily move back up on the seats to take a well-deserved breather through the upcoming pool. You are proud of your craft and you marvel at its ruggedness. You are aware that the number 5s and 6s require cool-handed control and experience.

This gentleman is either preparing for the rodeo or just intently interested in keeping his bow dry.

Before setting out onto the river, a few basic guidelines must be followed. First of all, you must be thoroughly familiar with your canoe and how to handle it. Paddling must be second nature. Secondly, you must be able to swim. And whether you're a poor swimmer or an Olympic champ, you must always wear a life jacket. Finally, something I've mentioned earlier, but something which bears repeating: Never go out on the river to run white water alone, and the first few times you try it, go with someone who has had plenty of experience.

Each time you launch the canoe, be sure it's on an even keel. I like to keep my bow just a fraction higher than the stern. Rapids are like a staircase, and the water runs down the hill over the steps. A slightly raised bow, in my opinion, gives better maneuverability, provides for a drier ride, and allows for less chance of tripping over a submerged rock (the "no-see-ums" of the river) and being swung sideways to the current. Caution should be taken not to shift the weight too far aft because that could cause another problem such as reducing the amount of draft forward and pushing the stern too deep. Too much weight in the stern could make the canoe very difficult to manage. If, however, the river passage is clear and straight ahead and the water is rough and swift, it might make for a drier passage to have your bow man shift to a position just behind the bow seat but not between it and the thwart (particularly if he's in the 200-pound category).

Sitting on the seats should be reserved for gentle passages and cruising, or just drifting along enjoying the ride. In white water, however, I like to be kneeling on both knees so that my center of gravity is lower and if I have to paddle myself out of a bad situation, I can get more purchase power on the paddle without rocking the canoe.

Always try to be alert to what's happening ahead of you. The bow man is in a good position to spot the "no-see-ums," and if you stay on top of things and pay attention to the signs, you should have no trouble picking your passage. It is im-

By controlling his slippage as he angles with the stream flow, the stern man guides his canoe preparatory to the next plunge down the river.

The bow man pulls as the stern man sweeps to bring the canoe around.

portant that both canoers become skilled in each other's position. It is good to switch positions but in real tough water, I always feel easier knowing the stronger paddler is in the stern. This in no way is meant to detract from the importance of the bow man who often must take the initiative and quickly swing into action and change course. The stern man must then scramble to bring his end of the canoe around. White water is a two-man effort and there is often no time to question. Each must have implicit faith in the other person's judgment, and whoever makes the first move, the other man must follow.

For your first adventure, do not exceed number 3s and even then be sure to check with the local authorities to be sure the river is not running higher than the ratings. It is not uncommon on many rivers for 3s to be running 4s and 4s to be running 6s.

It is important to stay to the outside of turns because that is where the water is deepest, although you may have to do some setting, which we'll discuss a bit later, to make the corner. The inside may look easier from a distance, but chances are it will be shallow, with gravel or cobblestones just under the surface. Small, uniform ripples would be a verification of this. Should you get into this kind of water by mistake, and run aground, simply get out of your canoe and walk it along to deeper water. In these shallow-water situations it is all the more important to keep your canoe on an even keel and level, thwart to thwart. When the bow is low and gets hung on a rock, there is every likelihood that the stern will swing around broadside to the current where you could possibly swamp.

If this situation should occur, the bow man can and should put one foot out and quickly shove off from the obstacle before the canoe swings sideways in the current. If you cannot get your foot on the rock and the water is more than a few inches deep and running swiftly, try instead to shift your weight and pull off with your paddle. If the stern hangs up, the same instructions apply but make sure also that you have on shoes that will give you good traction. What starts off as a minor hang-up can turn into a real troublesome situation and damage the canoe, so both canoeists should remain alert to avoid such situations. When you feel the stern swinging around broadside with the current, it is often best to get the canoe turned completely around so that the bow is facing upriver. You may save a dunking by doing this, and there is an excellent chance you can slide your canoe off the rock. It's not very graceful to go down the river stern first, but it is acceptable as a means of getting free. You should, however, get yourself into an eddy as soon as possible so that you can get turned around. Pick the first available one that will take you and paddle right on in by pulling forward.

If you wish to enter an eddy stern-first while going downriver, it would be best to proceed as follows. Try to imagine the standing waves in the middle of a stream flow as being similar to moguls on a ski slope. They stay in one spot, they

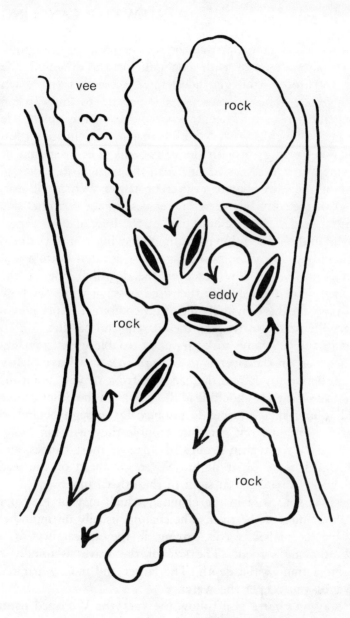

Using an eddy as a turnstile by entering into the back flow, making the turn, and shooting off at a better approach angle to the river below.

do not move. As you approach the standing wave from uphill, you will slow down as with a mogul. On the downhill side of the wave or mogul, you accelerate. Remember this when running white water, because it is important to know when backing into an eddy. Execute your move on the uphill side of the wave which is slower and where you will encounter less turbulence backing through the eddy wall. The execution of this maneuver was discussed earlier in the section on paddling.

Leaving the eddy is quite a different matter. When you exit, pull out of the eddy bow-first so that you hit the downhill side of the standing wave. It should pick up the bow of your canoe, which should be tilted downstream, and swing it into the current quickly. The water pushes against the tilted bottom and pushes it around. A low brace on the downhill side by the stern man holds the canoe in the tilted position while the bow man draws on the downhill side. The combined effort moves the canoe around smartly into the current and parallel.

One of the best ways to keep out of trouble when traveling with a group on the river is to be sure that you leave plenty of room between you and the canoe in front of you. Someone who knows the river should lead the way, and the other canoes should follow at a respectable distance far enough behind so that if the one in front gets into trouble they will not bump into it. Always travel in groups of three or more canoes, and never travel alone or at night. Never go ahead of the lead canoe, and always keep in sight of the other canoes.

The idea is to stay in the channel, which may or may not be in the middle of the river. The channel usually distinguishes itself by its higher waves, giving it the appearance of a swiftly moving serpent. The size of the waves is usually a good indication of the depth. The larger and more separated the waves, the deeper the water.

To stay on course you follow the vees, the V-shaped paths found between the rocks. Be aware, however, that the vee can close on you if there happens to be another rock in your path. You must be able to read signs quickly, especially if the rock

Driving toward the center of the open vee.

is under the surface of the water. Look for the turbulence marking an underwater obstruction, and remember that the actual obstacle will be some distance up the river from the sign, depending on the swiftness of the river. It takes time and experience to judge how far back from the turbulence the obstruction is, but it is an important ability which must be mastered. If you have to change course quickly, a push stroke or a sweep rudder action may be sufficient to set you on a new course. However, the most important fact, and it cannot be emphasized enough, is that the quicker and more accurately you can read the signs of the river, the more time you will have to react.

A careful look down the river and at the surrounding landscape should give you a pretty good indication of what to expect ahead. Fields on either side of the river and the absence of abrupt or steep banks and hills squeezing in toward the river usually indicate that there are no major drops ahead, particularly if the river remains wide. Be watchful for that smooth horizontal line across the river. If you think you see such a line, stand up for a better look. Determine whether it is in fact a dam, a series of ledges, or another run of rapids. As you notice the fields giving way to hills which extend to the banks, you will probably notice the river narrowing and flowing faster. Expect soon to find sharp bends and the telltale signs and sounds of swift water.

Begin looking for the correct passage down through the rapids. As mentioned earlier, the strongest current is usually an indication of where the deepest water is. If it is running strong and swift, it is sometimes referred to as the chute, and as you study the water closely, it appears as a length of rippling ribbon with waves that seem to remain stationary. These are the

Driving through a set of standing waves.

Driving headlong through a haystack.

standing waves, and their size indicates the amount of clearance you have under the canoe. The larger they are, the deeper the water and the more uniform and even they are, the more likely the bottom will be smooth.

When these waves become too large they break apart, or if side currents run into them or the current rushes into the slower water, they break up and form haystacks. As menacing as they may appear, about their only threat is to get you wet and fill the canoe. It doesn't take much water sloshing around in the bottom of a canoe to make it difficult to maneuver, so try to keep as dry as possible. To avoid the full impact of a haystack, you can take it on the side and save a good dunking. It's surprising how much water is contained in a good-sized haystack and you would swear it all wanted to ride in your canoe. When galloping over the standing waves, it is often advised that you quarter them, approach at an angle as you would the wake of a passing boat on the high seas. This makes for a softer and drier ride, but caution should be exercised when performing this maneuver, and care should be taken that the stern man maintains good control over the canoe's alignment. A quick crosscurrent can very easily spin you into a broadside position and that could mean trouble.

Setting and ferrying are two important maneuvers which were already mentioned as a solution to particular problems on the river. They can often serve as a defensive measure in other situations. As an illustration, I refer to a section of the Delaware River above Port Jervis, following a short stretch of number 5 rapids just above the Mogaup River entrance. You move along into a pool followed by number 4s just before the river bends sharply to the right. The main current follows the outside of the bend, and cross-surface currents from upstream press you close into the bank. Ahead of you, just after the

The Housatonic River at Cornwall Bridge, Connecticut. Canoe A tries to paddle around the bend but is pushed into the bank by the cross-currents. Canoe B, which is aware of the strong crosscurrents and obstructions, decides to negotiate the turn by setting. The heavy arrow indicates the channel and main flow.

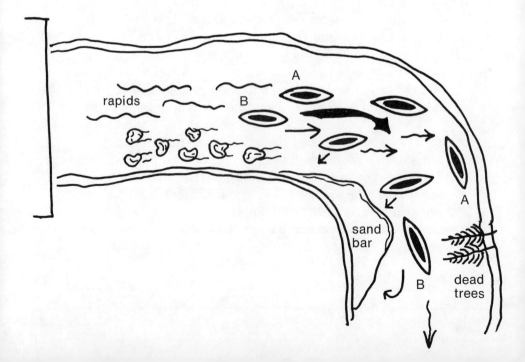

90-degree bend, are number 3s, and the crosscurrents continue from above, running straight on into the bank.

Unless you are prepared for a mad dash around the corner which could put you up against the bank, I would suggest that setting around a turn such as this might be a good alternative to a flat-out run. Simply keep the stern angled toward where you want to go and paddle backward. This will keep you high on the turn and out of trouble so that you can get into good alignment for the approaching number 3s. Such a maneuver is a form of setting, using the back stroke and angulation of the stern to the current as a means of sliding around the turn. Not very dramatic, but it gets you around.

Another good example of where this maneuver can work to your advantage is in an area of the Housatonic River below the covered bridge in West Cornwall, just before the river turns sharply right. As you come under the bridge, there is a

Paddlers are setting canoe around turn shown in illustration on page 102.

large group of cobblestones on the right. The water rushes through here at a pretty good clip. As you come out of the rapids and go toward the outside of the turn, you tend to forget that the water on the right is still moving straight ahead and forcing you into a steep bank that sometimes holds a few fallen evergreens that seem to reach out and try to grab you. Just beyond the turn is more white water. The water coming under the bridge on the right moves straight ahead and drives into the bank, moving whatever is on top of the water in with it. If, in situations like this, you still prefer to paddle around, you had better sink the paddle deep so that you have the advantage of pulling on the heavier channel waters bending around the turn.

A shallow area is another one of the annoying obstacles that you often find in your path, not particularly dangerous, but sometimes a real nuisance to get through, particularly if it crosses the entire river. It is caused by the river dumping deposits of gravel and sand, usually at a bend in the river where it widens or joins forces with another stream. It can be detected from above quite easily. The wave forms are small and close together. They are often referred to as "rifts," and the river is very shallow as indicated by the wave pattern. Sometimes the debris is so arranged that it develops a shallow falls. Often you will find large boulders scattered in among all this, some showing their faces above the water, others hiding just under the surface.

The best route through these areas is usually over toward the bank or at the outside of the turn. Sometimes this area is very narrow, and the water, constantly seeking more room to get around the bank, keeps digging and undermining the shore, eroding it away. Fallen trees caused by this action often add to the problem. Sections like this are always places where traffic jams can also add to the confusion, so it is a good idea to have the stern men get out in the shallows and hold their canoes back, allowing one canoe at a time to negotiate the passage.

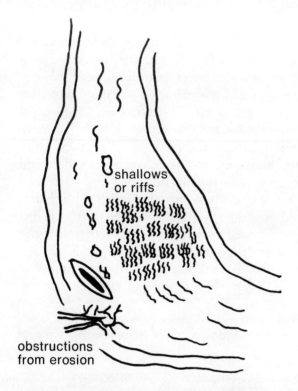

shallows
or riffs

obstructions
from erosion

A blanket of small turbulence waves indicates a shallow area of silt or cobbles, the appearance of water over a bar.

There always seems to be a desire on the part of new white-water enthusiasts, as they begin to feel their canoe moving down a rapids, to paddle faster. As the canoe accelerates over the surface, the paddlers pull harder. It makes for a thrilling ride when everything is going well. The obvious problem is that when you are moving at a high rate of speed over the water, stopping and turning become much more difficult. Travel at a moderate rate so that if you have to make a sudden change in course you will not have to spend so much time and energy slowing the canoe.

It should be mentioned here that, for all the fine attributes a canoe has, it is not without faults. One of them is its inability

to turn under certain circumstances without elaborate action
fore and aft. It is, in a way, like a slick destroyer on the high
seas. It can drive through the water at tremendous speed because it is long, narrow, and powerful, but it takes quite a bit
of effort and room to get it moved around in a high-speed
turn. The techniques discussed in the section on paddling cover
turns, slipping, setting, sliding, and pivoting. With these combinations, the canoe, unlike the destroyer, can be moved around
dramatically, especially with the aid of eddies and back currents. Several examples of these maneuvers have been presented. I will mention another turn which, when properly executed, can become a prized maneuver in your repertoire since
it involves a keen knowledge of river reading, judgment, and
control. It can be a grief saver if you have a sharp changeover

The water moves back upstream into the eddy behind this rock which
splits the flow of the river. Champion canoer Payson Kennedy presses
onward.

in the stream and not enough time to set yourself into an eddy stern-first.

Usually when conditions exist as illustrated below and the water is running fast, there is not enough time to set or ferry into an eddy. When the water is really moving, paddling backward can become extremely difficult because you are pushing the water in the direction it and your canoe are both going. The swift speed of the water does give you some compensating assistance by increasing the size of the eddy and providing a back flow of currents that could work to your advantage. You would still have to work through the eddy wall but, if there were a whirlpool effect, the wall would be negligible because where you would enter the eddy the slower moving water would be going in the same direction.

The key thing to keep in mind here is being able to judge, by the swiftness of the water, when to begin your move so that you will not overshoot your eddy and get into difficulties while the canoe is broadside to the current.

Driving down stream enjoying the ride.

A cool head, good training, and gradual experience are the best assets for handling the test of white water. In the early springtime, practice your paddling and review the guides and warning signs nature provides for reading the river. When the water is warm enough, practice capsizing and rescue techniques and, if possible, become affiliated with a club or group. Keep your body in good physical condition, and you will be able to confront with confidence the challenges of the river.

7

Canoemanship: *Weather, Map and Compass Reading, Knots*

Weather

ANYONE WHO HAS STUDIED the subject—pilots, navigators, and weathermen—knows that meteorology, the basic science of weather prediction, is highly complex, employing elements of physics, chemistry, and mathematics. Basically, weather is caused by the interaction of the air, the sun, and the movement of the earth. Here in the United States most of the weather moves across the country at a rate of between 500 and 700 miles a day from the West to the East. The earth, spinning on its axis, and the sun, heating somewhat differently the deserts, mountains, forests, and bodies of water, cause the formation of high- and low-pressure areas which, in turn, cause windshifts and various weather patterns. The complexity of weather reporting is often taken for granted. Not until you are canoeing, camping, or planning some other outdoor activity do you suddenly realize weather's importance and begin planning your activities according to the day's or week's forecast.

When you are on the river or the trail and happen to pull out your transistor radio for a weather report, you sometimes find how vague and inadequate these reports can be. From the quick one-liners they sandwich in between the jingles and the rock music, it is difficult to determine what tomorrow's weather will be.

Keeping in touch with the weather is essential, however, for both your safety and your comfort, so when you are living in the outdoors it is important to familiarize yourself with the many extraordinary early warning weather signs provided by nature. All you have to do is look about you and you can accurately determine what the weather is going to do. The clouds, the winds, sunrises, sunsets, dew, smoke, haze, visibility, sounds, leaves, and the behavior of animals and birds are all telltale giveaways of what the weather is going to be like.

Basically there are three types of clouds. Cirrus are the high, wispy clouds that look like thin, white brush strokes. Stratus clouds are long, trailing clouds that usually indicate fair weather. If they begin to bunch up at medium altitude, however, they could bring rain. Cumulus clouds, the ones you see on picture postcards, are usually low in the sky and look like cotton balls. There is nothing that can enhance a view more than a vivid blue sky with fluffy white cumulus clouds.

There are combinations of these types, and the manner in which they behave can foreshadow quite accurately, along with other information, what the weather is going to do.

Fair-weather clouds are, of course, the cumulus, but if they begin to show at higher levels as cirrocumulus, which are like fish scales uniformly bunched together in rows, it's a pretty good indication that unsettled weather or a storm is on the way. Fishermen often refer to this cirrocumulus formation as a "mackerel sky." Medium-sized cotton balls close together are known as altocumulus. They also indicate fair weather but usually do not last very long.

When cumulus clouds begin to cluster together and rise, it is almost a certain indication of thunderstorms and high winds. They usually begin forming in the Southwest early in the day, in most parts of the country, and grow increasingly menacing, towering into the sky with dark undersides. By afternoon, they usually have developed into cumulonimbus (nimbus meaning rain) and strike out with violence, high winds, hail, and lightning from the West or Southwest. Often they seem to be working against the wind, but when they approach with the wind there is usually little time to seek shelter. Get to shore and safety as quickly as possible. Avoid barren islands and high points of land, and never seek shelter under a tree. Stay away from metal sheds, metal canoes, and rock bluffs. Especially in New England, some rock is heavy with iron ore which greatly enhances the lightning's attraction for the rock. Be sure that the ground you seek shelter on has plenty of high trees which will make better targets than you, but do not get too close to them, and stay away from the larger ones, especially the oak trees. If there is no shelter, lie flat on the ground but stay out of puddles or streams. Water is about as good a conductor as

High, wispy clouds such as these are a sign of fair weather.

These uniform, fish-scale clouds signal the possibility of rain within twenty-four hours.

copper, so sitting in a stream would be comparable to sitting in an electric chair.

Stratus clouds which appear as dark smoky layers usually indicate a long period of rainy weather is approaching. Everything looks gray and damp because the sun is not visible. There

Low layers of clouds which can blot out the sun for days.

Though these are considered fair-weather clouds, you should be on the alert, when they are present, for a change.

are seldom high winds, violence, or lightning with these storm clouds, but rain can last off and on for days. Finally, as the front (pressure change) passes through, short squalls may occur along with fast-moving, low-flying clouds. This is usually

Fair-weather picture-postcard clouds. Most commonly found on travel brochures.

ABOVE: Cumulus clouds bunched together with dark underbellies can form into threatening thunderheads.

BELOW: Heavy cloud layers, dark and light in color and filled with rain. They move moderately fast and usually blanket out the sun for long periods.

an indication that better weather and sunshine are on the way.

Wind also is a pretty good indicator of weather change. Even the fish seem to be aware of a wind change or the phenomena that accompany it. If you have ever been around a salty old fisherman, you would be bound to hear him utter sometime, "Wind from the East, fish bite least; wind from the West, fish bite best." A rhyme not always true, I might add, but the fact does remain that when the wind is from the East, wet weather is ahead and it's a good idea not to be fishing around in a storm. This brings to mind another little morsel of seafaring rhyme: "When the wind is from the East it's just not fit for man nor beast." When a cool wind is blowing and the air is clear and boats and islands look as if they are standing above the water, you can be assured that a change in the weather is on the way. If you are near the ocean in the North where the tide changes are severe, this change will probably come with the change in the tide since the rising and falling of the water, according to some prognosticators, causes a change in atmospheric pressure. When there is a haze hanging over the water or land, the chances are pretty good that the weather will remain stable for awhile.

I have always heeded the old rhyme, "Red sky in the morning, sailors take warning; red sky at night, sailor's delight." I have never kept records but my own experiences would seem to support the fact that this method of forecasting is far more accurate than many a vague radio report.

Cows gathered together in a field also let you know that they think a storm is coming. Deer and other animals get the vibrations early and begin to come down off the high ground and head for the low lands. Gulls move inland if a big storm is coming, and the birds seem to become restless and appear to fly lower than usual. If, at night, you notice there is no dew on the ground, you can expect a shower or storm, possibly before morning. A heavy dew, on the other hand, indicates settled weather and a clear day. There may be fog in the morning, but the chances are good it will burn off long before noon.

When cows gather together in a field, rain is probably on the way.

"Rain before seven, clear before eleven." This is quite often true of showers unless the storm system is dense and widespread.

I recall one morning on the river when I watched everyone get soaked trying to prepare breakfast in the rain at about 8 o'clock. From my tent I had repeated the little rhyme, "Rain before seven, clear before eleven" several times but it went unheeded. I watched as they struggled to get the fire going and I later observed them munching on their eggs which had become bathed in raindrop gravy. I sighed, rolled over in my warm sleeping bag, and went back to sleep as the rain pattered gently on my tent. At 9:30 the sun was beginning to break through and by 10 o'clock the tents and the grass were nearly steam dried by the sun. I prepared breakfast and wished my rain-soaked friends as good a good morning as I could under the circumstances.

The leaves on the trees almost always will signal the approach of a storm. Since there is a pressure change preceding a storm, the leaves appear to reach up, showing their undersides. This can precede a storm by several hours and the warning can be verified by the clouds, the cows, or the wind. As a youngster I learned to pay attention to these warnings, but I was always impatient to get on with whatever I was doing, especially if I had been sailing or swimming. I always wanted to know how long the storm would last.

Old Captain Link Ford who, while I was a boy, could spin breathtaking yarns about the sea always seemed to be aboard his antique launch tied up at the dock when a storm was approaching. Sometimes, as he would sense our impatience at having to return to shore, he would take his pipe from his mouth just long enough to utter, "Short notice soon to pass; long notice long will last." We always appreciated his prognostications, and there was no one ever who could convince us that there was a better weatherman than our Captain Link. I still lobster and fish from the same little harbor and, although I have learned a lot about sighting and sensing the weather, I still find the uncanny wisdom these old salts seemed to have to be absolutely fascinating. Even today, with all our modern technology, I personally follow the advice of a lobsterman friend of mine, Carl Ford (no relation to the old captain), before I set out to check my traps.

At night when you are making camp and the smoke rises and blows away you can be quite sure that tomorrow will be clear. If it hangs heavy and low, expect rain. If suddenly the thought passes through your mind that the canoe trip you are on has improved your hearing, don't you believe it. Just accept the fact that the clearer sounds from the countryside or water about you are only an indication of a weather change and possible rain.

The noise of the locust will very accurately inform you

of how hot it is going to get during the day. Just listen to him;
the more noise and the longer he protests, the hotter it will get.
The crickets who mostly work the night shift can indicate
how cold the night is going to be. If you notice they are not
chirping, it's because the temperature is below 40° F. and they
are busy putting on their woollies and getting ready for a cold
night.

Smell also is more acute in the face of an impending storm.
I don't mean necessarily the smell of bacon from a distant
campfire, but more specifically the smell of swamps and animals. On numerous occasions I have been alerted to the presence of deer from their pungent odor, which is much more
pronounced in the face of a storm.

It is easy to take advantage of all the signs nature provides
for determining the weather, and it is important to learn them
for your safety as well as comfort. Contrarily, it is foolish to
defy the forces that the weather is able to unleash because
there is something very permanent about being hit by lightning
or drowning. I saw a friend of mine in school stand on a float
where we were swimming and wave his arms defiantly at the
sky as it unleashed bolt after bolt of lightning. The earth
seemed to shake from the thunder. Finally as we watched
fearfully from the shelter of the shore, he dived into the water
and was subsequently struck and killed.

Map and Compass Reading

It is important at all times to know where you are on the
river. If you have a good map, showing bridges, roads, islands,
and towns, you can use such landmarks to pinpoint your location. When there are no landmarks, however, and when the
river twists and turns, it is easy to lose track of where you are.
This is when a compass can be of help.

For river running and backpacking I like a compass that is

attached to a baseplate which serves as a direction pointer for taking bearings, as well as a ruler for measuring distances.

To find out where you are on the river, line yourself up, if you can, with landmarks, and move the map into a corresponding position. Check this out by orienting your map to the compass. Set the compass housing so that the needle fits into the North arrow frame, and be sure this is parallel with the North arrow on your map. Now set your base arrow (direction of travel) in line with the river. The compass reading in degrees where the direction of travel line meets the compass ring is the direction of the river at that given location. If you are lost, move the compass (being careful not to disorient the compass or the map) until the direction of travel arrow matches up with the river as shown on the map.

There is one more very important factor which must be considered, and that is variation, the difference between true North and North as registered by the compass. If the North arrow on your map indicates true North you must compensate for variation, since your compass indicates magnetic North.

Magnetic North, which is what attracts your compass needle, is in the vicinity of Prince of Wales Island, about 1,000 miles from the true North Pole. If you were canoeing on the Hamilton River in Labrador, you would have to add about 30 degrees to properly orient your map with your location. Your compass, here, would be reading 30 degrees West, or to the left of the true North Pole. On the Connecticut River your variation would be about 18 degrees; and, if you were canoeing through the Everglades, your variation would be O, because the magnetic Pole lies directly on a line from true North through the Great Lakes and Florida.

When canoeing to the west of this imaginary line, it is necessary to subtract rather than add the variation figure. For example, on the Colorado River you must figure on subtracting about 15 degrees to determine true North; on the Snake River, about 22 degrees.

Since variation changes slightly at different times of the year

and in different years, you may wish, if you are in the northern extremities (East or West) of the continent, to obtain a
variation and declination chart for greater accuracy. Another
problem could be deviation caused by the presence of iron or
steel around your compass. Do not take readings with your
compass near a belt buckle or knife and do not place it on a
rock. Take your reading where you are sure there will be no
interference from other magnetic fields.

Without a compass all is not lost. For emergencies nature
has provided us with the North Star which can easily be located in the sky by following a line from the bottom of the
big dipper through the lip. The North Star sits along this imaginary line about five times the distance between the star which
signifies the lip and the closest bottom star.

In the daytime if you want to find North it will be on the
scrawny side of evergreens where the branches are sparse.
More accurately drive a stick in the ground and point it at the
sun so there is no shadow. Wait a while and when the shadow
appears the end closer to the stick is West and the point of the
shadow will be East.

Do not underestimate the value of your compass; not just for

OPPOSITE PAGE: It is always important to know where you are on the
river. With the use of a map this is possible. If you were to arrive at
the old bridge as shown in the illustration, you could easily tell from
the map how far it was to the East Branch, to the town by river, and
to the town by land. Should you wish, for example, to purchase supplies at the town and continue on the left branch of the river, you
would have to travel four miles across country and then return. For
this journey you would be dependent upon your compass since there
are no roads, streams, or other landmarks indicated on the map. By
placing the compass on the map so that the pathfinder arrow points
toward the town you then rotate the compass housing so that North
on the housing is properly lined up with the magnetic needle. The
number of degrees (in this case 90 degrees East) which lines up with
the pathfinder arrow is the direction you must go to reach the town.
It is important that you check your readings and direction frequently
and carefully as you proceed.

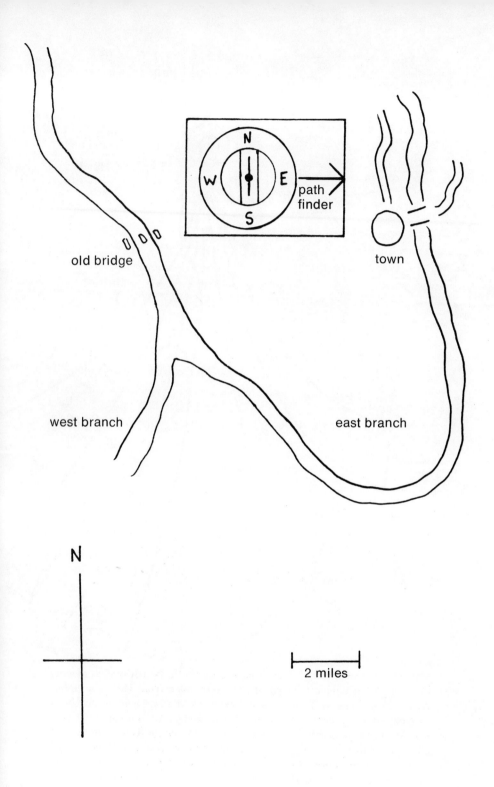

old bridge

path
finder

town

west branch

east branch

N

2 miles

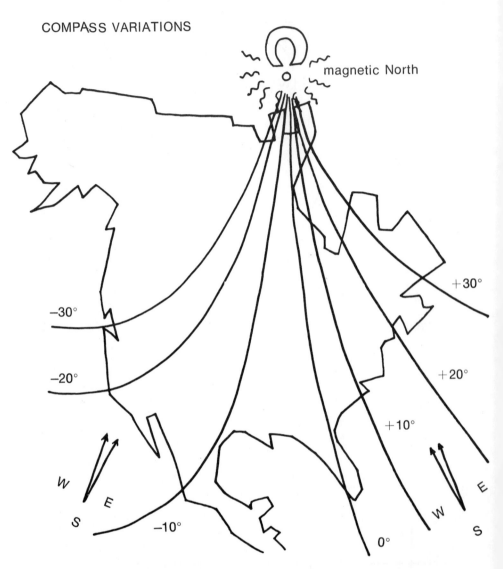

true North

COMPASS VARIATIONS

magnetic North

+30°

−30°

−20°

+20°

+10°

W
E
S

−10°

W
E
S

0°

Variation is caused by the fact that the magnetic North which attracts the compass needle is located about 1,000 miles from the geographic North Pole. Specifically it is near Prince of Wales Island in northern Canada, about seventy miles beneath the surface of the earth. Therefore, to find true north, if you were on the Delaware River, you would add approximately 12 degrees to your compass reading. If you were canoeing on the upper Ohio you would have little or no variation. If you happened to be in the West on the Colorado River, you would subtract about 15 degrees.

finding your position on the river, it will be a valuable aid in the event you must abandon the river and strike out across land which may be sparsely settled, if at all. To be prepared for this sort of event, it is wise to carry up-to-date maps of the entire area you are traveling, especially in wilderness areas.

Knots

Any type of boating requires some basic skill in knot tying. In canoeing, especially, properly securing your craft to the roof of the car is a vital procedure. On the river you must be able to tie lines properly in many situations. The basic knots shown here are sufficient to meet the various demands you will encounter.

TWO HALF HITCHES

This basic knot is simple to tie. The line is looped around a firm object and then looped over itself twice.

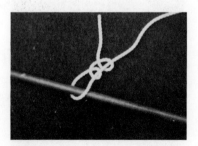

BOWLINE

A quick and easy way to make a loop that will not slip. This knot is often taught by describing the end of the rope as a rabbit which comes out of his hole, goes around the tree, and back in his hole again.

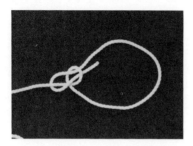

CLOVE HITCH

A quick way of securing to a post or spar.

FISHERMAN'S KNOT

A fast way to join any two lines together, even if they are of different size.

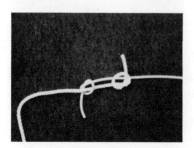

SHEET BEND

Also used for joining ropes.

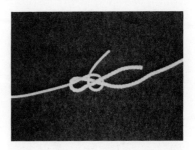

BUTTERFLY NOOSE

A secure jamproof loop that can be made in the middle of a line. You may want to have several. It is good for hauling, climbing, and in any situation where a loop is required where there is no end.

SQUARE KNOT

A quick knot that will come apart easily after use. Can be used for tying together odds and ends around camp.

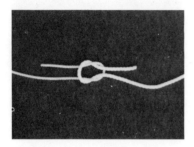

TAUTLINE HITCH

A versatile knot that can be tied while the line is under tension. By sliding the knot it is possible to tighten or loosen the line.

 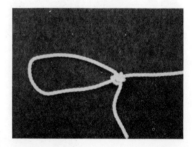

8

Coping With Emergencies

Rescue Maneuvers

IF YOU'VE EVER FACED an emergency on the river, you know the main reason whitewater canoeing should never be done alone. As I mentioned earlier, it is best to travel in groups of at least three canoes. You then have the necessary manpower to handle most any situation.

If you see someone in trouble on the river, stop and lend a hand. If it is someone other than a member of your group, pull your canoers into shore and plan what you can do to help. Do not move in immediately for a daring rescue, because the chances are that you, too, will end up in a bad situation unless you are lucky enough to find an eddy directly under the trouble spot. Unless you proceed cautiously and with a plan, it is quite easy to pile up an entire group of canoes and then it will take forever to get the mess untangled. Do keep in mind, however, that if the water is cold the body can function for only a short period of time. You must move with decisiveness.

If you are the victim of the river and everything is against you—you get hung up on the rocks, your stern is swung sideways into a boulder, and you fill with water—all is not lost. Your first move should be to make sure that in no possible way you allow yourself to get between the rock and the canoe. It would be like getting pinned to the wall by a locomotive. A swamped canoe holds about a ton of water and with the force of the water pushing against it, the downhill side of a canoe filled with water is no place to be. If, in the process of flipping over, you are tossed into the drink, don't panic and try to head immediately for shore if you are in the throes of turbulent water. Ride out the rough stuff with your life jacket by going down the river on your back, feet first, but pull out of the current and go to shore just as soon as you can do it safely.

Back at the canoe you may find that a tug or push with the help of the current may swing your swamped canoe back into the channel. By guiding it from the stern, it is entirely possible that you could rescue the canoe further downstream in calmer waters. If the canoe is loaded with gear, either get it to shore or let it float downstream, but be sure that it is spotted by someone in another canoe and rescued. If the gear has been sealed securely in large plastic bags, the air will keep it afloat and dry. If, after removing the equipment and with the assistance of friends, you still cannot get the craft to budge, there is another method which sometimes works when all others fail. If the water is not too deep or the current is such that you can stand with reasonable security on the bottom, place a line from the upstream end of the center thwart down and under and around your canoe. Pass the end of this line to two members

If it becomes necessary, always proceed downstream feet-first, guiding yourself by paddling with your hands. Fend off rocks with your feet.

of the rescue party who should take a position upriver from the canoe a few yards behind you. Standing upstream from the canoe yourself, place your feet on the gunwale and reach forward and pull on the far gunwale as you push with your feet.

When the canoe gets wedged against rock, first empty the contents, then try to work an end free. If this does not work, place the line around the canoe as described above. Next,

stand on the gunwale and grab the far gunwale with both
of your hands. By pulling and pushing with your feet, you
can sometimes walk the hull of the canoe up the rock and roll
it over. As the downstream gunwale rises, keep pulling so
that the water pressure does not cause it to slide back. A steady
pull and push will usually roll it over. Then it can be flipped
and refloated.

This method of rolling over a canoe usually works quite
well. If circumstances are such that the water is too deep, a
pull at an angle, with a line placed over the hull at one end
or the other and attached to the underside thwart closest to the
end of the canoe, may work. This one, to be effective, usually
requires the aid of a hand winch.

The canoe-rescue method which follows should be at-

A swamped canoe in deep water is no problem to empty. Here it is
being flipped over on its back.

ABOVE: The rescue canoe is steadied fore and aft by the paddlers as the swamped canoe is lifted up on the rescue craft.

BELOW: The canoe is worked forward until it balances with both ends free of the water.

Above: The canoe is rolled over toward the bow of the rescue craft. The men in the water assist as needed.

Below: The canoe, now right-side-up, is ready to go back in the water.

It is slid back into the water over the gunwale of the rescue canoe, then brought alongside for boarding. The entire procedure can be performed in less than a minute.

tempted only if, in your judgment, conditions prohibit moving a swamped canoe to shore, if the water is too deep to stand in, or if there is plenty of time before you will be running into more swift water. Unload the contents of the canoe that is swamped into another canoe (other than the one making the rescue, if possible). If the water is not too cold, let the paddlers hang onto the side of the third canoe. Come up alongside and roll the swamped canoe over on its back. Reach over and gently break suction, lifting the canoe off the surface of the water. Lift the canoe bottom up and over the gunwales of your canoe at right angles. When it is balanced across the gunwales, flip it over and let it slide gently back into the water. The crew now can enter from the water by the method that will be described shortly.

If you are faced with the problem of a swamped canoe, and a new set of rapids is fast approaching, you may be able to get a line from the swamped canoe to another canoe and paddle

ABOVE: In shallow water the canoe can be flipped in the following manner. One man gets under the canoe and lifts it free of the water.

BELOW: He then pushes up and starts the flip, taking care not to pick up any water.

swiftly to shore with it from where you can pull the swamped canoe in without losing ground to the flow of the river. If the river is shallow, you may be able to walk the rescue line to shore. If there is an eddy close by, you might head for that. If the eddy is shallow and fairly calm, you might consider flipping the canoe there.

It is possible to empty a canoe in deep water without the

With a final heave, the canoer lets go of the high side . . .

and the craft sits right-side-up on the water. As the canoe comes to rest right-side-up, grip it by the gunwale or painter so that it will not drift or blow away. It should also be mentioned that the canoe should only be flipped away from you downstream to prevent any possibility of being hit by the canoe as it is caught by the onrushing water.

aid of another canoe. By thrusting it forward and up, you can spill out the water a little at a time. When you have emptied most of it, you can enter the canoe and bail out the rest with the bailer you tied to the thwart. If you can touch bottom, roll the canoe over, duck under it and flip it. Be careful, before you heave, to gently raise one of the gunwales so that you can break suction and let more air in under the canoe. The more

By using a second canoe as a brace, a paddler can enter his canoe with-out fear of tipping it over on himself. Here the canoe is being held firmly while the man in the water scissor kicks and raises himself up to enter the canoe.

When he has risen to the full extent of his arms he must then reach across the gunwale and swing his leg up and over the gunwale into the center of the canoe.

An entry without assistance is done in much the same manner as entry with another canoe, except that greater care must be taken to balance the canoe so that it will not fill with water.

air, the easier and higher you can flip the canoe. As the canoe comes to rest right-side up, care should be taken to grip it by the gunwale or painter so that it will not drift or blow away. Also, you should always try to flip the canoe away from you downstream to prevent any possibility of being hit by it as it is caught by the on-rushing water.

There are two basic ways to enter a canoe from the water. The first is performed with the aid of another canoe. The canoes are placed alongside each other and the canoe that has lost its paddlers is held rigid by the occupants of the rescue canoe. The victim goes to the center of the far side of the empty canoe, grabs the gunwale there, and pushes and pulls himself over the side with the aid of a scissors kick. The other method of entering a canoe is by reaching across a single canoe with one arm and grabbing the far gunwale. Grip the near gunwale close to your chest. With your body straight and the aid of a scissors kick, work your body up over the side, taking care to keep the canoe balanced so that it will not take water. As you get your buttocks over the gunwale, twist and drop yourself into the center of the canoe.

Finally there are a couple exercises I would like to mention. They are taught at summer camps that have very rigid rules about moving around in a canoe. The first has to do with changing places in a canoe. To qualify as a canoer in some camps, you must be able to move from bow to stern and vice versa, even though you are instructed never to move around in a canoe. I do not recommend it, particularly if there is cargo aboard, and I don't know why you simply can't pull into shore if you have to change places. At any rate if you must, it works like this.

The stern man steadies the canoe while the bow man works his way backward to the center of the canoe without his paddle and assumes a sitting position. The stern man then stows his paddle and moves forward with his hands on the gunwales, staying low and being careful not to step on his

To enter the water from a canoe the paddler gets a firm grip on the gunwale and springs up.

While in the air he twists his legs up and over the side of the canoe, at the same time letting go of the far gunwale.

As he enters the water he maintains a grip on the canoe.

partner. He continues to move forward, kneels in the bow and steadies the craft while his, now probably wet, seated friend moves aft and takes his new position in the stern. I cannot for the life of me figure out why this is so important a requirement for the coveted canoeing award at summer camp, but it always seems to be part of the achievement test.

The other exercise that is taught at camp is how to go over the side. The reasoning behind this one is that you have to go over the side before you can practice how to get back in again.

It's also a good one to know if you have to go, over the side that is. From the seat of the canoe, free of the thwarts, grasp both gunwales, keeping your feet together in the center. Now support your weight on your arms and . . . alley oop . . . hike your legs over the side. Let go the far gunwale and check your entrance into the water with a scissors kick so that you do not spill the canoe. Oh, yes, you had better hold onto that canoe so it won't blow away.

Emergency Repairs

Most manufacturers have canoe-repair kits available. They consist of epoxy resins, aluminum patches with rivets, and other parts such as thwarts, bows and sterns, and decks. Wooden and canvas canoe manufacturers will send you new ribs if you tell them the number from the bow and/or the stern, and if you ask, they will tell you how to put them in.

If you are considering recanvasing your old wood-ribbed canoe which has been buried in the garage for a number of years, look into the possibility of doing it with fiberglass cloth. It is possible to get a 10 ounce fiberglass cloth in a 60 inch width which is perfect for the average canoe. You have no seam. You do not need a keel and you end up with a tough durable craft.

If you have a really badly banged-up canoe, check in with your dealer before attempting something you may be sorry for

later, especially with aluminum canoes. Canoes are very forgiving, but you should get advice before attempting a homemade job or before banging out completely a stove-in bottom.

The real purpose here is to discuss what to do on the river
where you might not be able to find a repair shop. Take along
a canoe first-aid kit which should have a roll of "duct" tape
and a rubber mallet. It is very seldom that you can't whack
back into floating condition even the sorriest-looking victim
of your poor judgment. For fiberglass and aluminum, especially, "duct" tape or "gaffers" tape, as it is sometimes called,
does a super job. It is waterproof and comes in large rolls, two
inches wide. On the standard size roll, which sells for about
$6 these days, you could tape a fleet of canoes and still have
enough for your home repairs. Once you have used this on
your canoe or around the house, you will never want to be
without it. It is manufactured by several different companies.
Some are imported. Stay away from these; they usually have
a shiny finish and they don't usually stick well to anything.
The good stuff has a dull finish and is dull silver in color. It's
tough and it's waterproof and sticks well, provided the surface
is dry. It can be used on tears, holes, leaky rivets, and just
about anywhere on the canoe.

If you are repairing a rip or a hole, first scratch up the surface and be sure it is dry before applying the tape. With
aluminum you may have to take out the dent first with a
rubber mallet. Lacking one, you can use the heel of your shoe.
Do your hammering against a backing of sand or water, and if
you have to pop out a large dent by a well-placed jump, do
it in shallow water, taking care that the canoe does not slip.
Rub up the surface with an ax blade or coarse sand, clean it
off and let it dry. Then apply the tape, inside and out. Cover
any sharp edges with the tape to prevent cuts or scratches to
your body. On a cold day, heat from a cigarette lighter might
help in the sticking on cold surfaces. Broken thwarts can be
repaired with saplings and duct tape and so can seats.

A rubber mallet is great for banging out dents and cuts, but more often than not repairs must be made without such tools because someone forgot the mallet. If damage is severe so that the ends of the broken metal must be brought together, do it gently with a cobble against sand or a rounded log. Do not try for anything more than bringing the surfaces close enough together so that they will support the tape. Too much pounding will weaken the metal and make a permanent repair later more difficult.

If the canoe is pressed hard against the side of a rock and swamps, the force of the water can split and cave in the entire side of the canoe. Using a life jacket to pad your back as you deploy leg power to the gunwale, the problem can be corrected. With the aid of tape and the addition of a thwart fashioned from a sapling, the craft can again be made seaworthy.

Do not try for perfection here. Bring the torn ends together with a minimum of pounding just enough so that they will receive the tape both inside and out. Try to eliminate jagged protrusions.

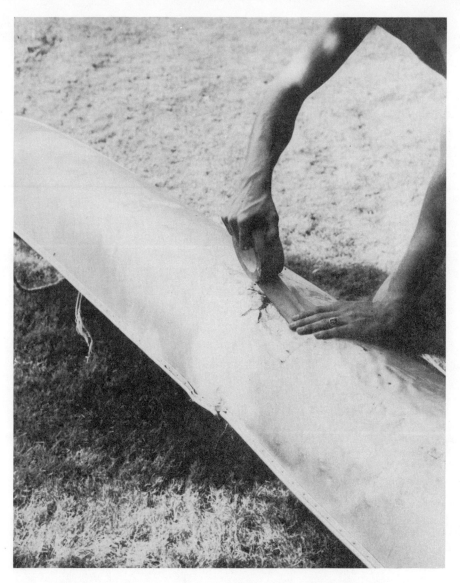

In applying the tape be sure that the surface is dry and free of dirt. If the weather is cold, heat the metal for better adhesion. Press the tape on firmly and use a liberal amount, both inside and out.

On long, extended trips you may elect to stop over a day to make more permanent repairs with epoxy kits and aluminum patches. These kits are available from manufacturers or marine supply houses and contain explicit instructions. Duct tape will work on canvas but you must prepare the surface well, getting all the varnish roughed before applying it.

Some of the things which are often overlooked on canoe trips are bailers and sponges to get rid of the water. Every book you read on small boat handling always mentions the importance of a bailer, but look around when you go whitewater canoeing and see how many you can find among the inexperienced. A bailer and a sponge should be a part of every canoe's equipment, especially when running white water. You are bound to take some water over the side, and if it can be conveniently scooped out with a bailer between rapids, it most certainly would save a lot of time and work pulling into shore and unloading, dumping out the canoe, reloading, and moving off again. An empty plastic Clorox bottle can be made into a fine flexible lipped bailer which you need for a canoe bottom. A piece of line from it to the thwart will keep it handy for use.

Emergency repairs can be made to a split paddle by using thin wire and boring holes on either side of the split with a knife drill and then, with the wire, lacing it like a shoe. It's a good idea to bore another hole at the top of the split about half an inch away, to keep the split from spreading. A broken shaft can also be repaired by winding the wire tightly around the shaft evenly from one side of the break to the other. This takes a lot of wire, and care must be taken to keep it even and tight. If you do not have enough wire, the same repair can often be accomplished with twine. If the shaft is snapped off, you will first have to splint it all the way around, keeping the splints close together so that they will not slip when pressure is applied to the handle. After the splints are tied in place for this repair, proceed to wind the shaft with wire or twine. If you had the time or were up a really long creek without a

A Clorox or similar bottle, cut as shown, makes an excellent bailer. The handle can also be used to tie the bailer to the thwart.

paddle, it would be possible to fashion one from a fallen tree
with the help of an ax or knife, or cut a 14-foot sapling and
try your hand at poling and snubbing. It's a good idea to carry
a sheath knife on your belt. It could become very handy, in the
event of an upset, to free cargo from a swamped canoe or even
yourself or someone else from tangled line.

I also like to see a painter line on every canoe fore and aft,
provided it is not loose. It can be stowed up under the deck
and held in place by a large rubber band around the coil or a
shock cord loop with wooden peg. The line can be quarter-
inch nylon. Always be prepared for the unexpected and proceed with care, and your repairs will be few. Above all, if you
do have a damaged canoe, try to repair it with tape. It should
get you home. I have never had to leave one behind.

9

Canoe Camping: *Food, Clothing, Equipment, and How to Pack It*

Food

THERE IS NO REASON why, when on a canoe trip, you have to eat dried food. Many books on canoeing claim that you should pack for a canoe trip as you would for a backpacking trip, traveling as light as possible and using freeze-dried foods. I disagree, unless you are going to be in the wilderness for weeks. First of all, some freeze-dried foods leave much to be desired, not only in preparation, variety, availability, cost, and taste but also in portions or amounts. After a strenuous day on the river, I could eat a week's rations of this type of food and be ready for seconds. That may be the reason I weigh 200 pounds, but I believe I can do just as well in the supermarket buying dehydrated foods and packaged meats. They're tastier, cheaper, and you can get as much or as little as you like and supplement where you choose with fresh foods.

I once took a group down the Delaware and served them a dinner that boggled their minds. It began with cocktails and dip, shrimp bisque soup and Caesar salad. The main course was porterhouse steak with baked potatoes and sour cream, and a delicious red wine, chilled in the river. A fruit compote and coffee followed by crème de cacao rounded out the meal. The background music for this riverside gastronomic delight was provided by the gurgling water singers that kept up the melody until we had all drifted off under a starlit night into dreamland.

Of course, this didn't happen every night but it was fun and, surprisingly enough, did not take that much additional preparation or, for that matter, that much additional space in the

Equipment for a two-day canoe trip. The total weight of the below items is about 32 pounds.

canoe. Coordinating a riverside adventure such as this is a bit of a trick, but with the help of my son, we managed to pull it off successfully, much to the delight of our guests, who I don't think will ever let us forget this banquet by the river.

Depending upon the duration of the trip and whether it will be taking place in a remote area, special consideration must be given to the type of foods taken. Here is a sample menu you can use as a checklist for your next two-day trip.

MEAL   TRIP #1. #2. #3.

SATURDAY BREAKFAST
At home or on the road.   ── ── ──

SATURDAY LUNCH

Packaged meat; black bread; cheese; Tang. ── ── ──

SATURDAY DINNER

Steak for two, cooked over an open fire
(frozen day before and placed in insulated
bag); frozen string beans; packaged soup;
squirt tube of oleo; cookies; dried fruit;
tea or coffee.   ── ── ──

SUNDAY BREAKFAST

Powdered eggs; bacon chips; black bread;
Tang; tea; coffee; cocoa or
instant tomato soup.   ── ── ──

SUNDAY LUNCH

Black bread; cheese and dried beef; dried
fruit, nuts, and raisin mix; Tang; tea or
instant soup.   —— —— ——

SUNDAY DINNER

At home or on the road.   —— —— ——

If you don't want to get involved with the frozen steak and
thermal bag for the first-night dinner, there is another quick
way of putting together an easy meal on the river or trail.
Using precooked instant rice as a base, add a concentrated mix
of any variety of packaged soup mix you prefer. It makes a
quick and nourishing rib-sticking stew or casserole dish.

If you're in a wooded area you can make use of natural
foods. The roots of burdock, cattail, and Indian cucumber are
all edible, as are hickory nuts, black walnuts, and hazelnuts.
Watercress and sorrel make excellent salads, and, of course,
there are the delicious wild strawberries, blackberries, rasp-
berries, and blueberries.

If you are on the river you should also be able to catch some
fish. There is nothing more delightful than to catch a few
fresh trout, clean them immediately, and then tie them to short
green sapling sticks. Poke the sticks, each with a fish, straight
down into the ground through the coals. With the fish heads
in the coals, let them cook for about ten minutes, and you
will have a pleasant gourmet surprise.

Clothing

Because many people can't think of canoeing in anything but a bathing suit, I thought it might be useful to include some information on proper attire for the river and cruising. This section might save you a great deal of discomfort since many writers tend to ignore, as the travel agents and picture postcard people do, the unpleasant little surprises that nature always seems capable of providing. Knowing how to cope with them makes them no more than minor annoyances.

The most important item for you to wear on the river is a life jacket. It is certainly necessary to be able to swim well if canoeing, but in white water the life jacket is absolutely vital. A stowed life jacket is of no use whatsoever in the event of a mishap, yet I know of at least one publication, conservative in some ways, which describes with photographs how to stow a life jacket in a canvas bag attached to the gunwale. The life jacket should be Coast Guard approved. The jacket which has the pillow behind the head and two buoyant sections on the chest is quite acceptable and reasonable. It gives you maximum freedom of movement, it's simple and comfortable, and it provides good protection for the head.

Life jackets that will not keep the head above water are useless, and can be dangerous. I almost lost my youngest daughter when she was only two on Compensating Reservoir in northern Connecticut. She was sitting in the water on the shore of an island and was toppled over by the waves created by a passing motorboat. She had a Coast Guard approved jacket on but her head went under as she struggled. Fortunately, we were close by and able to get her out quickly with no ill effects.

New on the market among life jackets is a Canoeist Buoy-

This sign placed above the bridge at Skinners Falls on the Delaware serves as a reminder to those about to run the falls.

ancy Vest featured by the L. L. Bean Company for about $20. It's Coast Guard approved, light in weight, has good ventila-

Rick Hudge, whitewater canoer and assistant manager of the Mountain Shop at the Outdoor Traders in Greenwich, Connecticut, displays several fine life jackets for canoers and kayakers.

tion, and provides excellent freedom of movement. It is one of the best I have seen for white water.

For any extended exposure to the sun or travel on the water, it is important to wear something over the thighs and shoulders. Long pants with room in the legs and a long-sleeved shirt with collar are best. The sun can do you in in very short order. If you simply must wear shorts, then at least drape a towel or something over your legs while sitting in the canoe. It will probably save you a lot of grief and pain. I know of one such instance where a friend of mine refused this advice and after two days on the river spent four days in bed with serious burns on his legs and ankles. He even has the scars to prove it. A hat that offers shade for the eyes and has a brim that will hold netting in case you run into black flies or mosquitoes is an item you don't want to forget. A fishnet-type T-shirt under your other clothing also makes it more difficult for these pesky critters to get a good bite. If you are accustomed to wearing sunglasses, by all means bring them along. The glare from the river can be pretty strong. Gloves that fit well for chilly days are also a good idea. They help, too, in the prevention of blisters while paddling.

One of the absolute essentials is a good pair of deck shoes. Be sure that the bottoms will grip well on wet surfaces. You must have good footing when standing on slippery rocks against the force of rushing water. Your footing must be firm when trying to extract a canoe from the rocks. Bare feet and slick-soled tennis shoes can only mean trouble. It cost a scoutmaster his life a few years ago when he slipped and struck his head on a rock and drowned while trying to assist someone in trouble on the Delaware. Practically all sneakers and tennis shoes (which are often suggested as good for canoeing) are potentially dangerous on the river unless they have a zigzag or locking grip, nonslip sole. As good as or even better than this is the felt-soled wading shoe or soft-soled moccasin. If you want, you can even buy, for around $6, a felt shoe kit from L. L. Bean. The felt sole is attached to your sneakers or

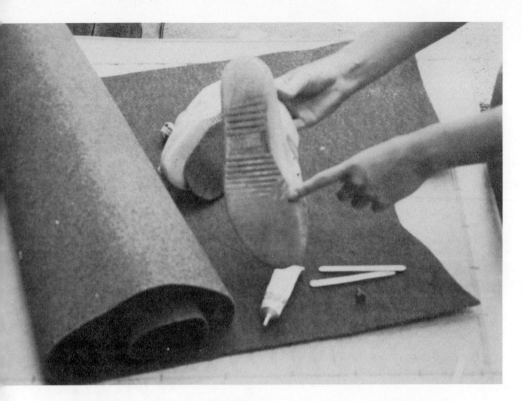

If you don't have the right footwear and are unable to find felt soles in a store, you can make your own non-slip shoes from a pair of slippery sneakers by using a scrap of indoor-outdoor carpet.

even to leather-soled boots. Punch some holes in the sides of your shoes to let the water out.

A new kind of garb that is fast becoming popular with whitewater canoers is the wet suit worn by skin divers. It is light, warm, and easy to move around in. If you do get wet with one of these on, the consistency of the material will still enable you to stay reasonably warm even though the suit remains wet.

If you do not have or do not wish to buy a wet suit, then be sure to wear wool longjohns in the early spring. Nowhere near as good as the wet suit, they nevertheless provide a certain amount of protection against the cold, even when wet.

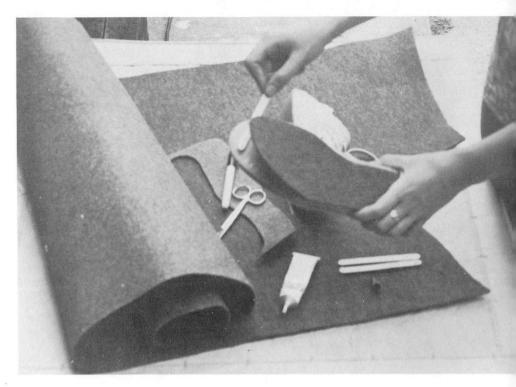

Apply the sole with a good waterproof cement, after roughing up the shoe. Cut the sole larger than you need.

Recent physiology reports claim that the maximum safe immersion time at a water temperature of 50° to 40° F. is less than ten minutes. Numbness and loss of muscular control will set in within about a minute or two, and the individual will be helpless.

For outer clothing I like a wool shirt rather than a sweater because of the pockets and collar. A water-repellent jacket is far better than a foul-weather suit which may keep the rain off but will cause you to become saturated in your own perspiration. It would be a very difficult struggle in white water should you get dumped, if you had on a foul-weather suit or even a poncho. Wear socks not only for warmth but to protect your ankles from the sun or rocks. Naturally you want to take along a change of clothing.

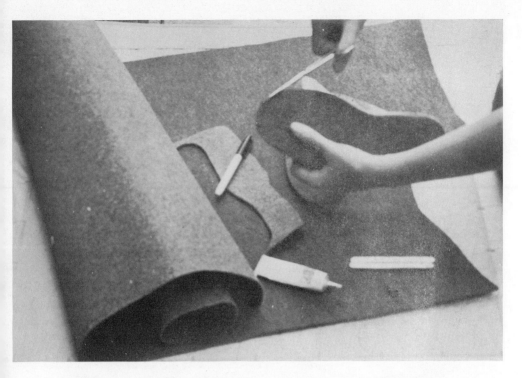

Press the sole on firmly after both sides have been covered with the glue. You can clamp it or press it, and when it is dry trim off the excess.

Another item we don't hear much about today is the bandanna, but it is still a very useful item to have along on a canoe trip or any other camping adventure because it serves many purposes. It can be used as protection from the sun around the neck, a bandage cover, sling, towel, strainer, sweatband, handkerchief, or a mosquito-control collar if repellent is placed on it. It can be washed quickly and takes but a few minutes to dry in the air and sunlight.

The most important consideration when it comes to clothing, especially in the spring and fall, is to have several layers that can be taken off or put on as the body dictates. I say "body" here because it is your normal body functions that can cause you grief on a cool-weather camping trip. Remember, it is your body that keeps you warm and it is the clothing you

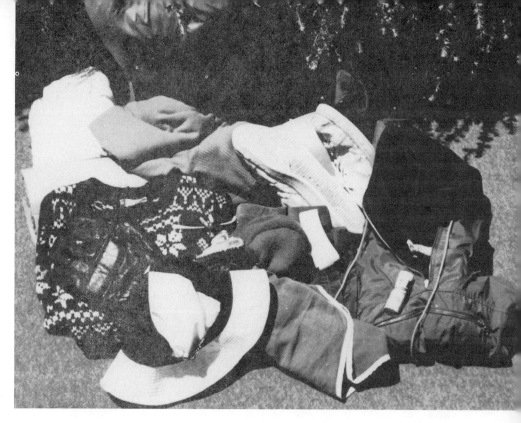

A complete supply of extra clothing. The above items weigh about 18 pounds.

wear that either holds in the heat or lets it out. If you keep a lot of clothing on while you are working or exercising, you will most certainly perspire, and if you have a nylon windbreaker on and zip up the front, this perspiration will saturate your clothing. When you slow down, the body will cool off and the damp clothing will bring you chills. Always pay particular attention to your clothing, and never allow yourself the misfortune of becoming overheated to the extent your clothes become wet and clammy.

In the summertime you must cope with another factor, loss of water from the body due to evaporation. Eighty percent of the human body is water. Dehydration of about eight percent results in dizziness or headache and can become serious. Three quarts of water are exchanged each day under normal conditions. About a quart and a half is lost through urine. Another quart is lost through the lungs, and about half a quart by evaporation or cooling of the body. This water loss could increase dramatically in the hot sun, so it is always a good idea in the summer to wear a light shirt, not only against sunburn, but to help retard perspiration evaporation on the body.

Knowing how the body chemistry works and how it must constantly react to extremes of hot and cold to maintain proper body temperature can be very important while camping or canoeing.

The list below is divided into two parts, what you will wear and what you will carry as extra with your bedding. In the early spring, you should seriously consider purchasing a wet suit.

CLOTHING TO WEAR   TRIP #1. #2. #3.

	#1	#2	#3
Longjohns (thermal or wool)	——	——	——
Wool shirt with pockets and long sleeves	——	——	——
Insulated socks	——	——	——
Deck shoes, soft moccasins, or felt fishing shoes	——	——	——
Long warm pants or shorts (but watch the sun)	——	——	——
Hat	——	——	——
Sunglasses	——	——	——
Gloves	——	——	——
Lightweight parka	——	——	——
Handkerchief and bandanna	——	——	——
Wet suit (a good idea for early-spring canoeing)	——	——	——

CLOTHING AND PERSONAL ITEMS TO CARRY

Life jacket (be sure it fits properly)   — — —
Wool turtleneck   — — —
Heavy sweater   — — —
Thermal socks   — — —
Pants   — — —
Longjohns   — — —
T-shirt   — — —
Shorts   — — —
Water resistant shell parka   — — —
Deck shoes or moccasins   — — —

Equipment and Camping Hints

A canoe trip, whether for only a few days or a week or more, should be an enjoyable as well as comfortable experience. It's a lot more fun to travel with a few extras that you would have to leave behind on a backpacking trip. I like the comfort and convenience of a good-sized tent with a floor, screened windows and entrance, and lots of good ventilation. With a tent of large proportions you can really enjoy a rainstorm and you don't have to be bothered with mosquitoes or black flies.

A down sleeping bag, while light and warm, can be miserable if it gets wet. If you plan on buying a sleeping bag, consider the new Fiberfill II®. It's du Pont's new polyester insulation fill; 1.4 pounds of this material equals a pound of goose down, and unlike goose down it doesn't ball up when wet. It even provides insulation when wet and can be wrung out and dried quickly. It is practically nonabsorbent.

There is no reason not to include a short-legged cot, a luxury air mattress, or even both. If you are traveling in a 16- or 18-footer with only your partner, there is plenty of room for these added items, and the difference it makes in the amount of paddling you will have to do is negligible. Be comfortable, have a good time, travel in comfort, and you can really recharge your battery instead of returning home exhausted, sleepless, and a prime candidate for a rest home.

Take along a big lantern, a couple of good books, or whatever makes you happy. Even a radio or television set if you feel, the first time out, you need some sort of a security blanket. This is beyond my own personal requirements, but I just wish to emphasize that if you feel the need for a few little extras, a canoe trip is the time to take them along. On the trail with a backpack there would be no way to carry such luxuries unless you were prepared to hire a squad of Sherpas.

I should reemphasize here the importance of a tent with floor and netting. Many books on canoeing show how to use your canoe as a shelter for the night, by laying it on its side and stretching a tarp or pine bows over it, forming a lean-to. This is a fine idea if you are sure there will be no black flies or mosquitoes around or, of course, in an emergency. Otherwise, it is an invitation to a sleepless night and a battle with the bugs.

All too often the brochures fail to mention the bugs. However, if you are prepared and can get dinner out of the way before the sun goes down, they will cause you a minimum of trouble. A small can of repellent is also good to have along. And, as mentioned earlier, if you really want to be prepared in a known bug-infested area, take along a head net that will fit over the brim of your hat. Wear a long-sleeved shirt and long pants, and don't forget socks unless you want the gnats to chew on your ankles.

If you like, you can also find room, on most trips, for a portable privy. A lot of river people would look down upon you if they knew you traveled with such extra comforts, but unless you want to take the time to arrange a suitable and comfortable half-moon oasis and then dismantle it and cover it over properly, a portable potty with a plastic receptacle, which is available through most large suppliers, is a wise convenience, especially when there are children along. The bag may be buried easily, and the frame seat folded and stowed. Your wife or friends might draw a limit to roughing it when it comes to such matters. To have your very own little potty is a lot better than having someone decide they can't go in the woods and then push through the bushes and walk three miles on a dirt road to the nearest highway in search of a gas station, only to find when they get there that the rest rooms are dirty and buzzing with flies.

Due to the recent assaults upon our country's well-known rivers, the state and forest services have had to impose restrictions. In some areas today the primitive privy trench is forbidden. Portable chemical potties are required unless the campsite is provided with the traditional half-moon "hoot-in-Annie." Remember, however, in the solitude of this single-hole privy, that you may not be completely alone. Always check under the seat to be sure there are no spiders lurking. Some species that dwell under privy seats are extremely poisonous, and if you are bitten by one of these culprits, you might not realize the seriousness of the bite.

When traveling on the river or lake, use care in the selection of your campsite. Stop early and when in the planning stage do not overestimate the distance you expect to travel in a day. Many guidebooks, such as the one published by the Appalachian Mountain Club, can be a big help here. If you are on the river, figure your distance for the day by mileage and the rate of flow. Don't find yourself having to paddle hard downstream because the river is running slow. Allow for stops or emergencies. If you see someone else in trouble on the river, by all means stop and lend a hand.

Most canoe rivers have publications which list campsites and provide maps of the river and other valuable information. Chapter 10 of this book includes addresses of several Eastern and national organizations that provide guidance for canoers. If you haven't made plans and are just meandering downriver, you can usually make arrangements to camp for the night with a local farmer along the shore provided, of course, that your group is not large and you won't have to keep running up to the farmer to get water or borrow something. A good point to remember, if the river is heavy with traffic, is that people with experience will be stopping early to get the choice campsites. Keep this in mind and plan to stop in the middle of the afternoon, at the latest, if there are lots of canoers.

I personally enjoy seeking out my own little campsite, away from the teenage drum band beating away on the bottom of their aluminum canoes. I don't like campsites where there is access from the highway and you end up sharing a skimpy plot of ground with parked motorcycles and a camper that runs its generator all night because the inhabitants have insomnia and spend the early morning hours watching the late, late show. There are such places as this and I mention them here only as something to be avoided. I also know of a fine, quiet site on the Delaware overlooking a beautiful stretch of river. Along about two in the morning, however, just over your head up the bank, a huge freight train rumbles by. Every 45 minutes or so you hear it again throughout the night. I have often wondered if possibly that wasn't the same train all night long and the engineer just couldn't find where to cross the river. Check your spot carefully, and you will have a much more restful night and feel a lot closer to nature.

When you pull into the bank for the night, be sure there is no possibility of your canoes floating away. Get them up on high ground away from the river's edge. After a good rainstorm or after someone has opened a dam upstream, I have seen people scrambling along the shore looking for their canoes that floated away in the night. Check the high-water mark on the bank and be sure to keep well above it.

If you plan to rough it and not use a tent, don't plan on sleeping under an aluminum canoe during a thunderstorm, unless you want to risk being fried by lightning. If you are pitching a tent, be sure that it is not perched high on a point poking into the air like a steeple. The view from this vantage point may be magnificent but you could be a prime target in an electrical storm. On the other hand, don't camp directly

A typical overnight campsite. Notice that the canoe is up from the water where the campers can keep an eye on it. In selecting a campsite the first consideration should be to make sure that you are well above the high-water mark. Try to locate a sheltered, dry high piece of ground where the air is moving. Be sure your canoe is secure and that your tent is pitched on soft level ground.

under a big tree. Try to find a sheltered location where there are, at a reasonable distance, higher targets for the lightning to flirt with. Beware of oak trees in an electrical storm. According to some authorities, they have about a 300 percent better chance of getting hit by lightning than do pine, ash, or maple trees. Of course, you certainly don't want to be on the river during a storm, so if one is imminent head for shore and either wait for it to blow over or make camp. Nothing is worse than trying to pitch a tent and make preparations for the night during a torrential rain or windstorm.

Usually it is quite easy to build your fire from driftwood except, of course, if there is heavy river traffic and camping spots are few and far between. If this is the case or if the weather has been wet, it might be better to go with charcoal or propane. Any good reliable stove will do. I personally do not care for the pressure gasoline stoves. I think they are messy and often require a lot of fussing unless you are completely familiar with them. They are like cameras. If you use them often, no trouble. Occasionally, it's another story. You must be completely familiar with them. For large groups I like the propane, if I must use a stove. Although the tank is heavy you don't have to worry about spilling gasoline or kerosene. Also the propane stove will handle two or even three rather large pots, and a small lamp attachment for the tank will provide an excellent camp lantern. This unit is good but also heavy. The three-burner stoves run about 35 pounds and, added to a 6-pound fuel tank and lantern, you will be carrying better than 40 pounds of cooking and lighting equipment. It is not

An overnight shelter fashioned from a space blanket.

always easy to get refills if you are in the wilderness, but the chances are there would be plenty of firewood in remote areas. Sterno, the small stove with the heat intensifier, is great for single portions or heating water for tea but impractical for a group. For individual portions, it is excellent for backpacking, provided you get the one with the intensifier. The black metal collapsible sterno stoves come with two burners, but are hardly worth the effort, unless they are well protected from the wind.

In the spring, when the ground is wet, it is a good idea to take along a package of dry tinder and then use the dead branches of hemlock or pine which you can snap off the trees.

When you are planning a canoe trip, find out what the requirements of the various campsites are, whether they are under control by some commission or club. During certain dry periods, for instance, the Wharton state forest rangers request that you use only stoves for cooking. This is becoming more and more of a requirement in publicly controlled camping

The Sandreuters pause for lunch on Connecticut's Housatonic River.

areas, so be sure to check ahead if you are planning to stay at one of these areas so you won't be disappointed and have to eat cold beans with bacon or steak, whatever the case may be.

It's surprising that on a canoeing trip the item most frequently forgotten about is water. On a hiking trip, water is always a concern, but when canoeing it never seems to cross one's mind because you think in terms of water all about you. Unfortunately, Coleridge's line from "The Rime of the Ancient Mariner" that goes something like, "Water, water everywhere but not a drop to drink," is often true. Our picturesque rivers are often too polluted to swim in, let alone drink from. Sad, but nevertheless true. I advise on river trips to take along five-gallon plastic containers for water. By "plastic," I mean the pliable kind that you can crunch down when not in use. They are rugged, they ride well in a canoe, and you can easily fit them in among the rest of your gear. They are currently selling for about $3. In a pinch, you can always boil water for ten minutes or use halazone tablets. If you use halazone, read the label. It usually states two tablets per pint and let the water stand 30 minutes. It is important to follow these instructions carefully.

Regarding food containers, bottles, and cans, the same rules apply to canoeing as apply to backpacking. Whatever you carry in, you must bring out. There is nothing worse than a load of empty beer cans clanging and dripping around in the bottom of the canoe. Fortunately for those of us who do not take kindly to those that guzzle their way down the river, we usually have a few allies among the insects. The yellowjackets love to ride in these canoes, and it's quite a sight to watch some greenhorn slobbering himself as he tries to avoid the yellowjackets buzzing around his lips and cans as he attempts to run the rapids.

In every three canoes, it is a good idea to carry along a 100-foot coil of dacron line. Also, a rubber boat fender (fairly heavy, yet tossable) for heaving. If you prefer, use a monkey-fist that will float or a baseball attached to a ball of strong nylon cord. The baseball can be thrown a considerable dis-

A small 14-inch boat fender tied to the end of a line and used for heaving and rescue.

tance with reasonable accuracy and upon reaching the victims in a river mishap, the nylon cord can be used to haul a heavier line for rescue. A word of caution: Anything that will sink will probably snag on the bottom when you try to retrieve it. With a small fender or the baseball, you at least have a fighting chance.

A couple of plastic water bailers, a couple of sponges, and a snake-bite kit are all good things to have along. I must admit I have never actually seen anyone get bitten by a snake, but on most camp trips they do present a potential threat. Rattlesnakes are found in every state except Alaska and Hawaii. New Hampshirites won't admit they have them, but a few have been known to make their way over from Vermont, or so say the Vermonters. Copperheads are found from New England to Kansas and on south to Florida and Texas. Water moccasins and coral snakes are only in the southern states, so say the northerners, but the best protection against them all is to be on the lookout for them and not to reach up onto ledges without first taking a look. Look before stepping over logs and generally keep your eyes alert for them. In the event of a bite, always treat it as if the snake were poisonous.

A first-aid kit is a must on every canoe trip. As a matter of fact, it is a good idea to have several if the group is large. Some member of the group should also be a qualified first-aider. Don't forget to take the first-aid book along also. There is nothing worse than a group of would-be experts differing about the treatment for an unfortunate victim. It's quite surprising, the various opinions some people have for treating such things as heat exhaustion and shock. A lot of confusion about how to treat the victim could cause him to panic, so if you think you may be a little rusty on your first-aid, bring along the booklet. It can be a big help when you are not quite sure about the proper treatment.

During the April-shower period and at other times, I have been known to produce a brilliantly colored umbrella from the bottom of my canoe. I get jeered at every time, and my children deny any relation to me. But as bizarre as it sounds, it does provide good protection in a cold spring downpour. There is something here to consider, however, and that is your attire against the rain while on the river. The thought frightens me, of riding through the rapids without my canoe, all tangled up in foul-weather gear or a poncho. You would be quite helpless in trying to protect yourself. That is why, even though I get the raspberry, I still prefer my bumbershoot. If, by chance, there is a breeze and it comes from behind, I get even with those critics when I change my bumbershoot to a spinnaker and glide off down the river while they are left behind to paddle through a sleepy pool.

The following list includes all the items you need for a complete canoe trip, be it of two days' or two weeks' duration.

The bumbershoot and rain. Admittedly it's more of a fun thing than a practicality. I really use it only to stress my disapproval of panchos and cumbersome heavy storm suits which can be a serious problem in the event of a capsize.

EQUIPMENT

TRIP #1. #2. #3.

Two-man tent   —— —— ——
Sleeping bag   —— —— ——
Sleeping mat   —— —— ——
Mosquito net   —— —— ——

Stove   —— —— ——
Fuel   —— —— ——
Matches   —— —— ——
Collapsible saw   —— —— ——
Sharp knife   —— —— ——
Cooking pot   —— —— ——
Frying pan   —— —— ——
Roll of absorbent kitchen paper   —— —— ——
Eating utensils   —— —— ——
Two plastic cups   —— —— ——
Two plastic plates   —— —— ——
Water jug with water   —— —— ——
Plastic jug for mixing juice, etc.   —— —— ——
Soap and scrubbies   —— —— ——
Toilet kit and any personal medications   —— —— ——
Lantern and fuel or batteries   —— —— ——
Flashlight   —— —— ——
Insect repellent   —— —— ——
Extra line and cord   —— —— ——
First-aid kit and booklet,
also snake-bite kit   —— —— ——
Bailers (two)   —— —— ——
Extra paddle   —— —— ——
Rescue line (50 foot) and throw
weight (fender)   —— —— ——
Metal signal mirror   —— —— ——
Duct tape   —— —— ——
Plastic bags   —— —— ——
Fishing line and hooks   —— —— ——
Portable privy   —— —— ——

Packing the Canoe

Most canoes, even the small 15-footers, are quite capable of carrying all your personal needs as well as tents and other

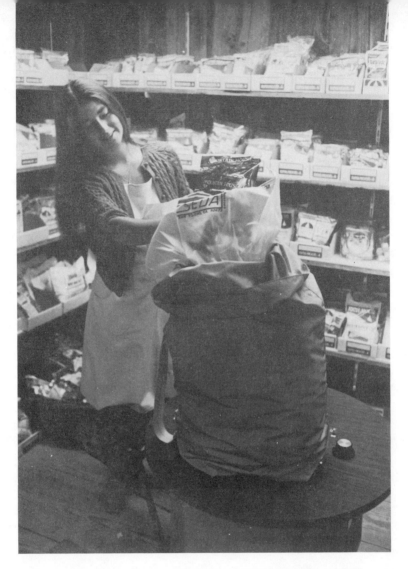

Chris Hugus, expert skier and member of the Outdoor Traders sales staff, fills a waterproof canoe bag with supplies from the Mountain Shop's dried food department.

camp equipment. In addition, most are able to carry three occupants. But with all this weight packed into a comparatively small craft, it's clear that everything must be properly stored.

Unless you are in the wilds where, for one reason or another, you might have to bushwack your way back to civilization, I would suggest that you leave the frame for your pack at home. Ideal for your personal things is a canvas duffel bag with either a zipper or draw-string opening. Packed in soft bags, your equipment will have no sharp edges, will be easy to stow, and will be easier and safer to put in double plastic garbage bags. I consider these plastic bags excellent for white water. Other waterproof bags are obtainable from outfitters, but they are expensive. Not only do the plastic bags keep things dry, but if they end up in the water they will float and can be retrieved by another canoe.

Here is a bag of clothing and food floating in plastic. Alongside is a snap lock plastic bag with a camera and wallet. This can be placed in a small canvas ditty bag and tied to the seat or thwart.

The placement of equipment is important. It must balance, should not be able to shift, and there should be room for the stern man to kneel and for the bow man to get behind the bow seat. The spare paddle is stowed against the side of the hull and tied to the thwart. If you are not concerned about the possibility of a wet canvas bag, place the plastic ones inside the canvas, load your clothes and equipment, seal the plastic, and zip the bag shut. I actually prefer this method, but for bags that have snaps or do not shed water well, the double plastic on the outside is better.

All of the equipment has been double bagged to protect it from the spray and keep it afloat in the event of a capsize. Keep all lines coiled and away from your feet and legs to prevent getting tangled. Tie anything that might shift, but make it easy to untie in case of a mishap.

Your personal belongings and the rest of your equipment should be balanced in the center of the canoe and secured so that the load will not shift. It is a good idea, after you get into the canoe with your partner and equipment, to be sure that your craft is riding even on the water. If it isn't, adjust the load. Leave enough room forward of the stern seat so that the paddler can get down on his knees and still have plenty of room to work the canoe. Room should also be left for the bow man to be able to kneel behind his seat in passages of heavy water. Nothing should be stowed forward of the bow seat except a short painter.

Your wallet should be in a small plastic bag and should be secured in either your shirt or pants pocket. Things like extra paddles, fishing poles, and push poles should be tied out of the way, but should be easy to break free. It is always best to use as little line as possible when securing your load. If possible, it is even better to use shock cords. If you keep your tie-downs to a minimum there will be less likelihood of your getting caught in a spider web of lines.

10

Places and Races: *Canoeing Trails, Camps, and Competitions*

THROUGHOUT THE UNITED STATES, there are thousands of miles of river trails and thousands of lakes beckoning you to enjoy them by canoe. Even within reach of our major metropolitan areas there are numerous picturesque canoe trails of varying difficulties and lengths.

A catalog containing one million miles of canoe and hiking trails is available from Ohio Canoe Adventures, P.O. Box 2092, Sheffield, Ohio 44054. In 1973, Stackpole Books of Harrisburg, Pennsylvania, published a book by Robert Colwell entitled *Introduction to Water Trails in America*. It lists hundreds of canoe trips throughout the United States, most within easy traveling of major cities. The book also includes information on how to get to the departure points, where to stay, and other pertinent facts about the rivers, camping areas, and canoes. For residents of the Northeast, the Appalachian Mountain Club of Boston, Massachusetts, has issued a *New England Canoeing Guide* which offers maps and listings of all the best navigable rivers of New England, with additional comments on campsites and other points of interest.

Several hundred canoe clubs and organizations are active across the country. Many of these are affiliated with the United States Canoe Organization, the American Canoe Organization, the American Whitewater Affiliation, the Sierra Club, and other national groups. There are organizations connected with schools and universities as well as with the Boy Scouts and Girl Scouts. All of these groups can assist you in becoming further acquainted with canoeing. Here are the addresses of the major canoeing organizations in America.

The American Canoe Association
4260 Evans Avenue
Denver, Colorado 80222

The American Whitewater Affiliation
Box 1584
San Bruno, California 94066

For information on specific states, you can write to the state's department of parks or department of public recreation. Area maps can also be obtained from the United States Geological Survey, Washington D.C. 20240.

As a fine example of good canoeing territory, consider the Rangeley District of the Maine Forestry Department, which provides 17 public campgrounds in the region. Many of these sites are accessible only by canoe or shallow-draft boat. A fee of approximately $2 is charged, and canoes can be rented for about $4 per day in the area. Further information may be obtained by writing the Campsite Coordinator, Maine Forestry Department, State Office Building, Augusta, Maine 04330. (Telephone: 207-289-2791.)

It is possible to arrange trips with registered Maine guides from Cupsuptic Lake in the northern part of the region down through Mooselukmaguntic Lake with a short portage around the dam into Richardson Lakes and on down for a distance of about 25 miles. Along the way there are numerous campsites and the area provides good fishing for landlocked salmon, trout, bass, and perch. There are also a number of private campgrounds in the region, and advanced reservations can and should be made. A list of private campsites is available by writing the Rangeley Lakes Chamber of Commerce, Rangeley, Maine 04330.

In New York State there are 154 state-owned islands on Lake George available to canoers. Although the lake itself is busy, it is possible to camp on islands small enough to permit only a single tent. Information and maps of the lake and islands are available from the New York State Conservation Department, Division of Lands and Forests, Albany, New York 12201.

Another Eastern area appealing to the flatwater canoeist is in New Hampshire on Lake Sunapee. There are many small streams and lakes nestled throughout the area north of Claremont, New Hampshire, which provide privacy and solitude, and a plentiful network of interesting streams which can be easily explored.

On the border between Minnesota and Canada are many magnificent wilderness areas where canoe-camping trips are featured by such outfitters as Olson's Borderland Lodge, Box 175, Crane Lake, Minnesota 55725 or Border Lakes Outfitters, Department D, Box 158, Winton, Minnesota 55796.

For the trip of a lifetime there is the 320-mile journey for the more ambitious and adventuresome canoer down Ontario's magnificent Albany River to Fort Albany on Hudson Bay. Tom Park, 22655 Marlin Place, Canoga Park, California 91307, runs two trips for wilderness buffs. One is in July for 22 days and there is an 11-day trip during the month of August.

For young men between the ages of 8 and 80 the Boy Scouts of America has recently opened a tropical canoe base near Inverness, in central Florida. The new facility is part of the 6,000-acre McGregor Smith Reservation and is called the Charles H. Topmiller Canoe Base. The area offers expeditions of up to 112 miles of year-round canoe trails on the Withlacoochee River System. The Topmiller Canoe Base is the fifth highest adventure scout camp in the states. Others are in Minnesota, Maine, and New Mexico. Facilities are limited, so trips should be planned well in advance by contacting the Director of Camping, South Florida Scouting, BSA, 2960 Coral Way, Miami, Florida 33145.

On the rivers, canoeing is growing so fast that at least one outfitter on the Delaware rents on the average of 400 canoes each weekend during peak periods of early summer. The popularity and increasing interest in the sport of whitewater canoeing has, however, created many adverse effects and problems.

Property owners, fishermen, volunteer firemen, and members of rescue squads, along with police and other public officials, are showing increasing resentment toward the sport, its participants, and those promoting and encouraging its growth and activities. Some volunteer members of fire departments and rescue squads along the rivers will tell you outright they simply do not like continually risking their own lives while some local outfitters who, in all fairness, do attempt to screen their customers, run no risks and gather in the money. The canoer is responsible for damaged or lost property and must leave a deposit to cover these losses. The abuse of private

The River Run Outfitters of Falls Village, Connecticut, is an excellent example of the complete whitewater center. In addition to outfitting canoers on the Housatonic, River Run offers advanced courses in canoeing and a kayak clinic, and each year operates several trips to the Rio Grande and Okefenokee.

property such as the cutting of trees and littering is evident most everywhere. Fishermen are constantly annoyed by the steady procession of sometimes noisy canoers who often without thinking charge through their favorite fishing pool and have been seen to toss their empty beer cans over the side. The fishermen too often defiantly hold their ground in the middle of the only safe passage. These situations do create problems which tend to dampen the enjoyment of all parties concerned.

Fortunately most people who canoe the Delaware, one of

the most popular and heavily traveled whitewater rivers in the
East, do carry their litter with them and dispose of it properly
at the end of their journey.

Having examined various natural campsites which exist on
state-owned property along the shore, I have frequently found
evidence of careless campers. However, I do get the feeling
that most people are policing the areas after breaking camp, and
I must say I believe that conditions are getting better, though
there is still a lot of room for improvement.

I am distressed by what appears to be a goodly portion of
alcohol consumed on the river. Whether the consumption is
heightened by the thought of falsely bolstering one's confidence or whether it's a means of warming one's innards, it is
as dangerous to drink while canoeing as it is to drink while
driving.

It also makes it downright unpleasant for those enjoying
the wonders of nature and the challenge of its forces when
a group of booze-bellied weekend canoe freaks charges by and
you eventually end up spending the afternoon fishing them
out of the water.

It appears to be a fact that in some areas the number of
drownings is increasing in alarming numbers. According to
reliable sources, 19 people have been killed in canoes, kayaks,
rafts, and inner tubes on the Chattooga River where the movie
Deliverance was filmed. Many times these unfortunate in-
cidents are caused by underestimating the forces of the river
and overestimating one's ability to overcome the hazards. Some
people consider it beneath them to wear life jackets, and they
often have inadequate equipment and a very adequate supply
of alcohol.

There is no escaping the fact, however, that the increase in
river running is cause for concern along our nation's picturesque waterways. In some areas it already has become so great
a problem that government agencies have been forced to regu-
late usage of such rivers as the Colorado and the Snake. Reg-
ulatory river-usage legislation is being considered in many

other areas of the country, to preserve and protect both the shoreline and the canoers.

It is difficult at times to realize fully the awesome responsibility even the experienced canoer is taking when he invites a friend to share the thrills and excitement of white water. More often than not, one's attention is focused on the pleasures derived from previous experiences and not much thought is given to the possible hazards. It is understandable that you would play down the hazard to your friends so as not to worry them. It can be startling to realize your responsibility to those that have put their trust in you and in so doing have, in effect, made you responsible for their safety and life. It is only fair that you require of them some knowledge about what they are about to undertake and that you do not take them beyond what you consider the limit of their ability. These are thoughts which are rarely given the consideration they deserve. Unfortunately, the full impact of precautionary measures is sometimes not fully felt until after a tragedy, at which time it is too late. One must always keep in mind that when you enter the rapids it must be with knowledge, confidence, and the ability to put it all together.

You are committed. There is no turning around, stopping, or falling down. You must, if you are to survive, make it through to the end of the run.

Fortunately, from Maine to California, canoe schools and canoe camps are more popular than ever. Many of them are offering excellent instruction and complete canoeing vacations.

One that deserves attention as a model for all others is in Wesser, North Carolina and operates twelve months out of the year. Payson Kennedy, well known outdoorsman, and canoe racer in the Southern Appalachian Mountains, runs a rather unique camp school and lodge known as the Nantahala Outdoor Center, situated on the Nantahala River. With his family and an impressive staff of canoe experts, he teaches the art of canoe and kayak handling, backpacking, and the preservation of our natural environment. The center is located on

Route 19, about 13 miles southwest of Bryson City, North
Carolina, where the Appalachian Trail crosses the Nantahala
River, considered by many to be the best canoeing river in the
nation.

The Cherokee Indians named this beautiful river and its
surrounding country Nantahala, "Land-of-the-noonday-sun,"
and it has been selected as the permanent site of the South-
eastern United States Canoe and Kayak Championships.

Kennedy, who is a former Georgia Tech professor and the
holder of several degrees, has been active in scouting and
possesses a deep concern for our natural environment. At the
age of 43, with his wife and four children, Payson headed north
from Atlanta in 1972 to the magnificent mountains of North
Carolina, just over the Georgia border.

From the remains of a failing restaurant and motel he and
his family, in just a few years, have developed this complex
into one of the most needed and welcomed whitewater canoe
operations in the country.

As Payson can tell you, it was not easy getting started, but
the Nantahala Outdoor Center and its excellent training programs are being recognized throughout the country. Here
clinics are planned to meet the needs of paddlers of all types
of boats, at all levels of skill. His staff includes members of the
National Canoe Team and former Olympic Team members.
Among them are such names as Les Bechdel, Ramone Eaton,
Russ Nichols, Lynn Ashton, and Louise Nichols. Aside from
a wide variety of year-round courses the Center can provide
all equipment for river trips, whether by raft, canoe, or kayak.

Life preservers, paddles, bailers, experienced whitewater
guides, as well as food supplies, are available. The Center requires that life jackets be worn at all times, that no alcoholic
beverages be carried on the river, and that proper footwear
and clothing are worn on all trips. On the Chattooga trip, helmets are furnished and must be worn. During the cooler
months wet suits are recommended and are mandatory during
the winter season. A limited number of these suits are available

at the Center. They can be purchased or rented. Lodging at the Center is available in the motel unit, and the Nantahala dining room, aside from its excellent food, provides a magnificent view of the Nantahala from large picture windows directly over the river.

A favorite run which can be enjoyed by even the most inexperienced is negotiated over an eight mile stretch of river through the spectacular Nantahala Gorge in 12-foot rafts and ending in a breathtaking ride over the Nantahala Falls. A well trained guide accompanies each group of rafters.

There are many other trips available at the Center including guided raft expeditions on the Chattooga River. Every precaution is taken by the Nantahala guides to insure a thrilling adventure rather than a dangerous ordeal. A guide accompanies the three paddlers on every raft. The most dangerous rapids are scouted in advance, and the guides provide instruction for negotiating the run. To assure a minimum of delays and a maximum amount of instruction per training period, one instructor is assigned to every five students in the clinics.

Open canoe clinics are scheduled each month from April through October. Decked boat clinics are scheduled each month from March through November. The goal of these clinics is to bring all participants to a level of skill which will enable them to paddle with safety, confidence, and comfort on rivers up to class 3 difficulty in the company of an experienced group.

Participants who have reached this level of proficiency may then concentrate on specific skills such as water reading, eddy turns, rolling, and braces.

The instructions for these clinics usually begin after dinner on Friday evenings with lectures and demonstrations on equipment and river safety. Saturday and Sunday are spent on the river where instruction is received in strokes and water reading. Saturday evening is devoted to a critique and period for questions and answers. Instructional films are also shown and a new one filmed especially for the program is underway, parts of

which are already in use in the program. The fee for this weekend clinic is presently $50.

Other programs are of a week's duration and include trips
on such rivers as the Raven Fork, Oconaluftee, Tuckaseigee,
Little, French Broad, Nolichucky, Tellico, and several others.
There are beautiful fall color cruises in October. The average
fee is $150 which covers all meals, lodging, and transporta-
tion costs.

Both three- and five-day courses for scouts are available. All
participants in these programs must have completed First Class
swimming requirements and upon the completion of both
courses they will have fulfilled all the requirements for the
canoeing merit badge.

The three-day course includes basic skills, safety and rescue,
whitewater techniques, river reading, and repairs. Also, teamwork and maneuvers. All equipment including knee pads, life
preservers, safety ropes, and repair and first-aid kits are provided.

The cost is $30 per scout for the three-day course with the
maximum group charge of $360. Two instructors accompany
each group.

The five-day scout course, in addition to the above, includes
an overnight trip on the Chattooga River. The cost is $10 per
day per scout with a maximum charge of $600 for 12 scouts.
Groups larger than 18 cannot be accommodated since it is
difficult to adequately supervise large groups.

There are additional activity packages offered at the Nantahala Outdoor Center and they include kayaking, combination
backpacking and canoe trips, and horseback trail riding.

The Center operates year round but the whitewater training
program does not get into full swing until early March and
continues until the end of November.

Aside from the excellent instructional program Payson Kennedy offers at Nantahala it is a place where novice as well as
expert can find plenty of enjoyment and excitement. There is,
in addition to the motel and restaurant, an outfitter shop and
grocery store. There is a repair shop and family cottages with

kitchenettes that can be rented by the day or week. Further information can be obtained by writing the Nantahala Outdoor Center, Star Route, Box 68, Wesser, North Carolina 28713.

Hopefully the programs offered by the Nantahala Outdoor Center will serve as guidelines for other centers across the country.

Competition

The challenge of white water, as with any exciting, fast moving sport leads eventually for many to competition. Downhill and canoe slaloms have long been popular in Europe and international competitions have been held for years. The Germans in 1972 chose, as the hosting country, to incorporate whitewater canoe competition as a special feature of the 1972 Olympics. A special course was actually built near the Olympic site and water from a nearby river was diverted through the course to make one of the best whitewater canoe runs ever. The water volume could be controlled by valves at the upper end so that each canoe experienced equal difficulties as it threaded down the demanding course.

For years Europeans have taken canoe and kayak racing very seriously, training long hours and searching constantly for new paddle techniques and river skills. It is only recently in this country that canoe racing can now be claimed as a more than minor attraction. Slalom competitions are held frequently throughout the country and are sponsored by various clubs and the American Canoe Association. The races are governed by the rules of the International Canoe Federation.

It is unfortunate, especially after the interest stimulated by the 1972 whitewater races at the Olympics in Munich, that the Olympic Committee and/or the Canadian government could not find a way of continuing what proved to be one of the most exciting and interesting events of the games.

As mentioned earlier, competitions are held throughout the country from early spring until fall. The most important event in the East takes place on the West River in Jamaica, Vermont. It is here that the Eastern Kayak and National Canoe Championship slaloms are held each May.

For those not familiar with the sport of canoe racing, a whitewater slalom is somewhat similar to a ski slalom. The races take place in single slalom kayaks, two-man kayaks, C₂ canoes, which are decked over with individual cockpits for the two occupants, and open canoes, which are raced solo or with a two-man team. The idea is to navigate through a series of control gates over difficult terrain through swift moving water in the shortest time possible.

The gates are pairs of poles suspended just above the water on taut cables stretched across the river. Approximately 15 to 25 gates are placed on a course which averages about half a mile in length. The gates are about 18 feet in width and are strung so that the competitor must thread his way through, sometimes by reversing, paddling back through an eddy, or driving through a series of heavy standing waves. Penalties are imposed on those canoers who fail to pass through a gate and/or touch a pole.

The penalties are severe with ten seconds being subtracted from the elapsed time for every pole touched. For a gate missed but touched on the outside by the canoe or paddler, the penalty is 50 seconds as opposed to 100 seconds, the price one pays for missing a gate completely.

It is interesting to notice the steady increase of spectators at these whitewater events throughout the East. It is interesting also to note the many fine new developments in boat design that have blossomed forth from these events.

As in skiing, the new and more effective equipment is very much in demand and because of the growing interest in competition more people are paying more money for the more sophisticated equipment being offered by sporting goods stores and canoeing shops.

A whitewater team drives hard through an open gate on the Nantahala River in North Carolina.

During the summer months races are held throughout Maine for beginners as well as experts. The Dead River serves as the scene for many of these competitions, including the Maine Open Championship which takes place over the Memorial Day weekend. In early May, Campton, New Hampshire, plays host for the New England Slalom Race and in late May, New Hampshire hosts the New England Wild Water Races as well as the SACO River weekend. In Connecticut, the Housatonic White Water weekend gets underway in late May. The Frost-bite Slalom in West Hartford, Vermont, which is considered by many to be the largest beginners slalom in the country, is one of the final races of the season. In Virginia each year a series of championship races are held which range from white water to flat water slaloms. These events usually take place at the end of April and information about them can be obtained by writing Canoe Races, P.O. Box 1291, Front Royal, Virginia 22630.

Beyond the actual competition of running white water is another extremely popular hobby, that of constructing one's own canoe or kayak for competition.

The search for extra strength and a lightweight craft that is highly maneuverable and will charge without faltering through heavy water forces serious-minded whitewater competitors to spend weeks on end during the off-season building new and better crafts. The tricks of the trade are many and varied. In the effort to build a seaworthy craft that will withstand the most violent of rivers, you can construct yourself a craft which, because of its strength, actually becomes dangerous. It is conceivable that a kayak could become pinned against a rock and the weight of the water could press the boat together enough to trap its paddler. Preferable in a situation of this sort would be a boat that would break apart, freeing its occupant. So the struggle is to provide the optimum of strength as well as safety. Numerous articles appearing in such magazines as *Down River* and others provide excellent information about materials and methods of construction.

Catalogs may be obtained from such outfits as Defender Industries in New Rochelle, New York, which sells polyester resins and fiberglass cloth as well as tools. Plasticrafts, Inc. of Denver, Colorado, also stocks the necessary material and offers a catalog for those interested in the art of canoe and kayak building. Molds are available for rental at a surprisingly reasonable fee and with a good set of instructions and the advice of those that have done their own building, it is possible to become deeply engrossed in a new and interesting avocation.

A new book by Charles Walbridge with lots of illustrations describes how to build fiberglass canoes and kayaks. It contains a great deal of valuable information about how to get started, what sort of materials and tools are required, and helpful advice along each step of the way in construction. Your whitewater canoe supplier should carry this book or know how to order it.

Canoeing is growing steadily throughout the country and the nice thing about this sport is that everybody can enjoy it. Those who seek relaxation and solitude can find it on the quiet lakes and streams in the back country. Those who seek adventure and excitement can find it on our swifter rivers. For those who seek competition, there are races just about everywhere where there are swift, moving rivers.

There is something for everyone on our lakes and rivers and you do not have to be a super athlete to be a participant. There are even such bizarre outings as the ones held by the Collinsville Connecticut Raft and Beer Society (CRABS). These events, which take place over several weekends in May, draw as many as 35 competitors with homemade rafts. There are specifications for the rafts, and participants must wear life jackets. The part that bothers me is the entry fee of one case of beer per raft. It is not that I am against beer, and events such as this sound like lots of fun, but I do wonder where the empty cans end up. Also, I have never felt that beer and canoes mixed any better than beer and automobiles, and I shall let it rest there.

Thoughts and Things

Of course, only experience can really help you do what's right on the river at all times. It is easy to describe how to free yourself from a rock or turn the canoe in an eddy, but until you have actually tried it, done it, you really can't appreciate all that is happening. Riding the river is not easy. You must be quick, efficient, and wary of the dangers before you. You must be in good shape physically, your mental attitude should be favorable to white water and you must have a desire to canoe.

Athough you don't have to train as you would for football or hockey, you should get in shape for canoeing as you would for backpacking. Walking, swimming, moderate exercises for arms and legs, a knowledge of what you are undertaking, plus the desire to succeed can open up entire new vistas of pleasure, understanding, and closeness to nature.

I have felt at various times throughout this book that the descriptions of what it is like riding through the white water and the emphasis placed on rescues, hazards, life jackets, and the importance of knowing your canoe and doing well, could have a decisively dampening effect on the enthusiasm of any-one attracted to the sport. True, there is danger in whitewater canoeing, and I would not feel comfortable if I felt I had led someone to think otherwise. In any sport, there are moments that call for decisive action and split-second timing. It is not uncommon for some to become nervous and tense in the face of a difficult whitewater passage. Panic can arise in an emer-gency and it can become difficult to react or think clearly un-less you take a quick appraisal of the situation and plan a way out of your predicament. When you begin to think clearly, the problem doesn't seem to be half as bad as it first appeared, and the panic and shock begin to subside. This is the reason that conditioning, both mental and physical, is important. Knowing you can go over in the thick of the water and still recover is half the battle.

As I mentioned in the preface, the inspiration and incentive for writing this book was motivated by what I found so often to be true, the great complacency and ignorance that goes with so many sports. As a ski instructor for many years in Vermont, I saw complacency and ignorance take their toll on the slopes. They take their toll each year among small boat owners, back-packers, climbers, and even swimmers. Overconfidence, lack of particular knowledge, and disregard for others account for thousands of deaths each year on our nation's highways, too. In fact, most anything we do in life can be dangerous, even

My father and son put it all together on the Housatonic.

changing a lightbulb or going down stairs. What is important is to understand thoroughly what you are doing, be aware of your limitations, and have concern for those about you.

A man and his canoe become a part of nature. It is right for them to be together. There is excitement in rushing white water, the solitude of a silent pool, or gliding along the banks of a slow-moving stream watching a weasel prepare his meal. There is splendor in watching a forest spring to life as the gray face of dawn gives way to the warm, rich colors of nature's bloom. A man in his canoe knows all of this, as well as the magnificence of sunset on a remote, still lake. He has heard the echoing sound made by the tapping woodpecker and he has seen the cautious deer make its way to the water's edge. He has smiled as the chipmunks dart about him and spy from behind trees. He knows of the great evening chorus, where insects sing in harmony with the gurgling waters, accompanied by peepers and deep-throated frogs.

These are the reasons for canoeing. A canoe can take you to places no other boat can reach, through God's forests and among his creatures. You feel small and humble as you see spread out before you all the wonderments of nature and life's great cycle. You are in attendance at the greatest symphony of all, the symphony of life and natural things. You see it performed exactly as it has been for centuries, and even though you must return to man's plastic world of neon lights, asphalt, and soft drink cans, you go a better person for you know where the real world lies, and you can always get there in your canoe.

Glossary

ABEAM
that portion of the boat or canoe which constitutes the side, and along side of which or adjacent to there lies an obstruction, craft, or body of land. This object is referred to as being abeam.

ABS-FOAM
a new resilient fiberglass sandwich material used in the construction of canoes. Air pockets within the material provide flotation.

AFT
toward the rear, in nautical terms.

BAGGED

materials such as food, clothing, and sleeping bags properly prepared and stowed in waterproof plastic bags for whitewater passages.

BEAM

the width of a boat at its widest part.

BOW

the front end of a boat. The end of the canoe where the seat is closest to the center of the canoe.

BRACE

a paddle thrust against the water with the face of the paddle used to steady the canoe.

BROACH

the turning sideways of a canoe toward the flow of water.

BROADSIDE

crossway to the current and flow of water. An undesirable position to be in and difficult, in turbulent water, to control.

BUTTERFLY NOOSE

loop knot used at bow of canoe for lining. It is a secure loop that cannot shift or jam and can be made in the center of the line or wherever necessary. Good also for rescue, hand holds, and climbing.

CANOE

a craft lower in the middle than at the ends along its gunwales or deck. It is usually paddled or poled. It is narrow in width and by contrast fairly long in length.

CHANNEL

deepest and usually the most canoe-able route down a river.

CHUTE

usually a fast and turbulent moving body of water, compressed through a narrow passage by rock ledges or river banks.

DROP

a descent in the river accompanied by rapids and riffles.

DUCT TAPE

silver, waterproof cloth tape, usually two inches in width on 10-inch rolls, used for emergency repairs on all types of canoes.

EDDY

an area downstream of an obstruction or along the bank where the water flow is circular or reverses to flow in an upstream direction.

EDDY WALL

the short turbulent waves which result from water flowing downstream against slower water moving upstream.

FACE

that portion of the paddle which is used to pull through or brace against the water.

FALLS

a drop in the river over which water falls free.

FERRY

a lateral movement across the current at an angle maintained by paddling upstream either forward or backward.

FREEBOARD

the portion or amount of hull exposed from the gunwale to the water.

GRADE

angle, slope, or drop of the river.

GRIP

the uppermost portion of the paddle held in the hand.

GUNWALES

the rail or uppermost portion of the side of the canoe which provides strength around the edge of the entire canoe.

HAYSTACK

large standing waves caused by sudden slow-up of water. They look large, white, and menacing but are usually filled with both air and water.

HEAD WIND

wind blowing directly at the bow of the canoe.

HEAVY WATER

unusually heavy flow, standing waves, or turbulence.

KAYAK

a small canoelike craft usually decked over and paddled with a double paddle.

KEEL

the lateral support piece which runs externally from bow to stern and provides the craft with strength and rigidity.

LEDGE

rock stratus which causes short dams or falls.

LEEWARD

the side of an island or boat not being hit by the wind.

LINE   correct name for rope used around canoes for tying, anchoring, or lining.

LINING   the process of working a boat upstream or downstream by use of lines.

PAINTER   a short line attached to the bow or stern of a canoe used to secure the craft to shoreline or dock.

POOL   a section of river, slow-moving and deep.

PORTAGE   the process of carrying a canoe over land.

RAPID   a series of waves or turbulence caused by water running rapidly down a grade over obstructions.

RIBS   vertical pieces of wood or aluminum that provide the canoe with strength and shape.

RIFFLE   a shallow section of river where there is an abundance of little waves bouncing over gravel or sand.

ROCKER   the curve of the canoe bottom from the center forward and aft.

SETTING   a ferry where the stern is angled upstream and the canoe is paddled in reverse.

SHEER | the upward curve of the hull from the center to the bow and stern.

SHOCK CORD | elastic line often used to secure gear in the canoe.

SHOE KEEL | a flat strip which runs the length of the canoe bottom in place of the conventional keel. It is preferred for white water.

SKIRT | spray shield which snaps to bow of canoe or cockpit of kayak.

STANDING WAVE | a wave that appears not to be moving and which accompanies a slow-up of current.

STERN | the back end of the canoe. The seat in the stern is nearer the end of the canoe as opposed to the bow seat which is closer to the middle of the canoe.

STROKE | method of movement for paddling a canoe through water.

THROAT | portion of paddle above face or blade that meets the shaft.

THWARTS | braces or cross members which extend from gunwale to gunwale in a canoe.

TRIM | proper angle, obtained by shifting weight, which canoe sets to best negotiate waves, wind, and current.

Tumblehome

the incurve from the keel to the gunwale of a canoe.

Way

movement through water by the canoe.

Wet Suit

a garment of neoprene sponge which fits close to the body and provides insulation against the cold water.

Windward

the side of the canoe, vessel, island, or shore which bears the full brunt of an approaching storm, wind, or sea.

Yawing

the zigzaging back and forth of your craft when being towed, or the resulting action because of too much weight in the bow.

Yoke

a molded device, or one fashioned from paddles, used to support a canoe on the shoulders for portage.

Index